Contents

Acknowledgments

Jessica Semega with the valuable guidance of **Bruce H. Webster Jr.** prepared the income and earnings sections of this report under the direction of **Edward J. Welniak Jr.**, Chief of the Income Surveys Branch. **Alemayehu Bishaw** prepared the poverty section under the direction of **Sharon Stern**, Chief of the Poverty and Health Statistics Branch. **Charles T. Nelson**, Assistant Division Chief for Income, Poverty, and Health Statistics, Housing and Household Economic Statistics Division, provided overall direction.

The report has been produced through the efforts of a number of individuals directly responsible for the design and implementation of the American Community Survey, including **Douglas Hillmer**, **Todd Hughes**, **Ken Dawson**, **Anthony Tersine**, **Nancy Torrieri**, **Deborah Griffin**, and **Alfredo Navarro**, as well as through the efforts of many Census Bureau staff working on the American Community Survey.

B. Dale Garrett, under the supervision of **Karen E. King** of the Decennial Statistical Studies Division, conducted sample review. **Alfredo Navarro**, Assistant Division Chief of the American Community Survey Statistical Design, provided overall direction.

Additional people within the Census Bureau also made significant contributions to the preparation of this report. **Marjorie Hanson**, **Leonard J. Norry**, **Cynthia Davis Hollingsworth**, **Scott Boggess**, **Ana J. Montalvo**, **Jennifer Day**, and **Barbara Downs** reviewed the contents. **Anika Juhn**, **Marc J. Perry**, and **Steven G. Wilson** provided technical assistance. **Matthew W. Brault**, **Victor M. Valdisera**, **Grace L. Clemons**, and **Cody A. Pfau** provided programming assistance. **Kirby Posey** and **Ashley Provencher** provided statistical assistance.

Census Bureau field representatives, telephone interviewers, and data processing staff collected the data. Without their dedication, the preparation of this report or any report from the American Community Survey would be impossible.

Corey T. Beasley, **Donna Ruuskanen**, **Theodora S. Forgione**, and **Diane Oliff-Michael** of the Administrative and Customer Services Division, **Francis Grailand Hall**, Chief, provided publications and printing management, graphics design and composition, and editorial review for print and electronic media. General direction and production management were provided by **Claudette E. Bennett**, Assistant Division Chief, and **Wanda Cevis**, Chief, Publications Services Branch.

Suggested Citation

Bishaw, Alemayehu and
Jessica Semega,
U.S. Census Bureau,
American Community Survey Reports,
ACS-09,
*Income, Earnings, and Poverty
Data From the 2007 American
Community Survey*,
U.S. Government Printing Office,
Washington, DC,
2008.

**Economics and Statistics
Administration**

Cynthia A. Glassman,
Under Secretary for Economic Affairs

U.S. CENSUS BUREAU
Steve H. Murdock,
Director

Thomas L. Mesenbourg,
Acting Deputy Director and Chief Operating Officer

Arnold A. Jackson,
Associate Director for Decennial Census

Daniel H. Weinberg,
Assistant Director for ACS and Decennial Census

Susan Schechter,
Chief, American Community Survey Office

Howard R. Hogan,
Associate Director for Demographic Programs

David S. Johnson,
Chief, Housing and Household Economic Statistics Division

Income, Earnings, and Poverty Data From the 2007 American Community Survey

INTRODUCTION

This report presents data on income, earnings, and poverty by detailed socioeconomic characteristics for the United States, states, and lower levels of geography based on information collected in the 2006 and 2007 American Community Surveys (ACS). A description of the ACS is provided in the text box "What Is the American Community Survey?"[1]

The U.S. Census Bureau also reports income, earnings, and poverty data based on the Current Population Survey Annual Social and Economic Supplement (CPS ASEC). Following the standard specified by the Office of Management and Budget (OMB) in Statistical Policy Directive 14, the Census Bureau computes official national poverty rates using the CPS ASEC and reports the 2007 data in the publication *Income, Poverty, and Health Insurance Coverage in the United States: 2007.*

The 2007 ACS is the second year of the survey's implementation

including both housing units and group quarters in its sample.[2] The ACS is designed to provide detailed estimates of housing, demographic, social, and economic characteristics for the states, counties, places, and

other localities. This report makes state-level comparisons over the 2006 to 2007 time period. Such comparisons should be interpreted with caution because of overlapping income reference periods.[3]

---

[1] The text of this report discusses data for the United States, including the 50 states and the District of Columbia. Data for the Commonwealth of Puerto Rico, collected with the Puerto Rico Community Survey first introduced in 2005, are shown in Tables 2, 5, 6, and 10; in Appendix Tables A-1, B-1, and B-2; and in Figures 1, 2, 3, 4, and 5.

[2] From 2000 to 2004, the ACS was in the demonstration phase, which consisted of a housing unit sample of approximately 800,000 addresses per year and produced estimates for the United States, states, and essentially all places, counties, and metropolitan areas with at least 250,000 people. In 2005, the ACS went to full implementation with its sample of housing units. The 2005 ACS produced annual estimates for the United States, states, and all places, counties, and metropolitan areas with at least 65,000 people. The 2006 and the 2007 ACS samples also included people in group quarters. For guidance on comparing 2007 ACS data with 2006 ACS data and data from other sources, see <www.census.gov/acs/www/UseData/compACS.htm>.

[3] As described in the text box "How Is Income Collected and Measured in the 2007 ACS?" the reference period for income data collected in the ACS is the past 12 months. As ACS data are collected in every month of the year, adjacent years have some reference months in common. Hence, comparing the 2007 with the 2006 estimates is not an exact comparison of the economic conditions in 2007 with those in 2006. Although the ACS will show trends over time, precise year-to-year comparisons are difficult to interpret. For a discussion of this and related issues, see Howard Hogan, "Measuring Population Change Using the American Community Survey," *Applied Demography in the 21st Century,* Steve H. Murdock and David A. Swanson eds., Springer Netherlands, 2008.

What Is the American Community Survey?

The American Community Survey (ACS) is the largest survey in the United States, with an annual sample size of about 3 million addresses across the United States and Puerto Rico, and is conducted in every county throughout the nation (including every municipio in Puerto Rico). As part of the 2010 Decennial Census Program, the ACS has replaced the traditional decennial census long form. The ACS collects detailed social, economic, housing, and demographic information previously collected by the decennial census long form, but it provides up-to-date information every year rather than once a decade.

Beginning in 2006, ACS data for 2005 were released for geographic areas with populations of 65,000 and higher. In 2008, the first set of multiyear period estimates will be released for data collected between January 2005 and December 2007. These 3-year period estimates will include geographic areas with populations from 20,000 and up. The Census Bureau is currently planning to release the first 5-year period estimates in 2010 for the smallest geographic areas—down to the tract and block group level—based on data collected between January 2005 and December 2009.

The data contained in this report are based on the ACS sample interviewed in 2006 and 2007 and include only geographic areas with populations of 65,000 and higher. For information on the ACS sample design and other ACS topics, visit <www.census.gov/acs/www>.

Additional historical trend data on median household income and poverty from the CPS ASEC are available on the Internet.[4]

The Census Bureau also produces annual estimates of median household income and poverty for states, as well as for counties and school districts, as part of the Small Area Income and Poverty Estimates program (SAIPE). For more information about estimates for smaller geographic areas, see the text box "Additional Source of State and Local Estimates of Income and Poverty."

This report has three main sections: household income, earnings of men and women, and poverty. The income and poverty estimates in this report are based solely on money income received (exclusive of certain money receipts, such as

[4] See <www.census.gov/hhes/www /income/histinc/inchhtoc.html>.

Additional Source of State and Local Estimates of Income and Poverty

While the ACS produces annual single-year estimates of income and poverty for counties and places with population of 65,000 or more, the Census Bureau's Small Area Income and Poverty Estimates (SAIPE) program produces single-year estimates of median household income and poverty for states and all counties, as well as population and poverty estimates for school districts. These estimates are based on models using data from a variety of sources, including current surveys, administrative records, and personal income data published by the U.S. Bureau of Economic Analysis. In general, the SAIPE estimates have lower variance than the ACS estimates, but they are released later because they incorporate ACS data in the models. Estimates for 2005 are available on the Internet at <www.census.gov/hhes/www/saipe /index.html>. Estimates for 2006 and 2007 will be available later in 2008.

capital gains) before deductions are made for items such as personal income taxes, social security, union dues, and Medicare. Money income does not include the value of noncash benefits such as food stamps; health benefits; subsidized housing; payments by employers for retirement programs, medical, and educational expenses; and goods produced and consumed on the farm.

How Is Income Collected and Measured in the 2007 ACS?

The information on income and earnings presented from the 2007 ACS was collected between January and December 2007. People 15 years and older were asked about income for the previous 12-month period (the reference period), yielding a total time span covering 23 months. For example, data collected in January 2007 had a reference period from January 2006 to December 2006, while data collected in December 2007 had a reference period from December 2006 to November 2007.

All income was inflation-adjusted to reflect calendar year 2007 dollars. That is, the 12 different reference periods were adjusted to reflect a fixed reference period, in this case January 2007 through December 2007, using the Consumer Price Index (CPI). This adjustment took the sum of the 2007 CPI monthly indexes, divided by the sum of the CPI monthly indexes for the income reference period, and multiplied the result by the income.

Example: Consider a household surveyed in June of 2007 with a household income of $40,000. The sum of the CPI monthly indexes for 2007 was 3,653.7. The sum of the CPI monthly indexes for the reference period June 2006 to May 2007 was 3,589.4. Dividing 3,653.7 by 3,589.4 creates an adjustment factor of 1.0179. Multiplying the reported household income of $40,000 by this adjustment factor results in a 2007 inflation-adjusted household income of $40,716.

For more information on income in the ACS and how it differs from the Current Population Survey Annual Social and Economic Supplement (CPS ASEC), which also collects information on income, visit <www.census .gov/hhes/www/income/factsheet.html> or <www.census.gov/hhes/www/poverty/acs_cpspovcompreport .pdf>.

For a comparison of median household income data from the ACS and the CPS ASEC, visit <www.census.gov /hhes/www/income/newguidance.html>.

HOUSEHOLD INCOME

Household income includes the income of the householder and all other people 15 years and older in the household, whether or not they are related to the householder. For comparisons of household income, this report focuses on the median—the point that divides the household income distribution into halves, one half with income above the median and the other with income below the median. The median is based on the income distribution of all households, including those with no income.

In the 2007 ACS, information on income was collected between January and December 2007. All income data were inflation-adjusted to reflect calendar year 2007 values and are referred to in this report as 2007 ACS income. See the text box "How Is Income Collected and Measured in the 2007 ACS?" for more information on data collection and income adjustment.

Median Household Income for the United States by Race and Hispanic Origin[5]

The discussion of race groups in this report refers to people who indicated only one race among the six categories in the survey: White, Black or African American, American Indian or Alaska Native, Asian,

Native Hawaiian or Other Pacific Islander, and Some Other Race.[6]

In the 2007 ACS, median household income in the United States for all households was $50,740.[7] Table 1 shows that Asian households had the highest median household income ($66,935). While not statistically different from each other, the median household incomes for Native Hawaiian and Other Pacific Islander households ($55,273) and

non-Hispanic White households ($55,096) were less than that of Asian households and higher than that of Some Other Race households ($40,755). American Indian and Alaska Native households ($35,343) and Black households ($34,001) had lower median household income than the other race groups. Median income for Hispanic households was $40,766 in the 2007 ACS.[8]

Median Household Income for States

Table 2 shows the median household incomes of states from the 2006 ACS and the 2007 ACS. The median household income estimates in the 2007 ACS varied from state to state, ranging from a median of $68,080 for Maryland to $36,338 for Mississippi.[9]

Table 1.
Median Household Income in the Past 12 Months by Race and Hispanic Origin: 2007

(In 2007 inflation-adjusted dollars. Data are limited to the household population and exclude the population living in institutions, college dormitories, and other group quarters. For information on confidentiality protection, sampling error, nonsampling error, and definitions, see *www.census.gov/acs/www/*)

Race and Hispanic origin	Median household income (dollars)	
	Estimate	Margin of error[1] (±)
All households	50,740	75
White alone	53,714	109
White alone, not Hispanic......................	55,096	106
Black alone	34,001	208
American Indian and Alaska Native alone............	35,343	714
Asian alone	66,935	465
Native Hawaiian and Other Pacific Islander alone.....	55,273	2,660
Some Other Race alone	40,755	270
Two or More Races	44,626	610
Hispanic (any race)	40,766	182

[1] Data are based on a sample and are subject to sampling variability. A margin of error is a measure of an estimate's variability. The larger the margin of error in relation to the size of the estimate, the less reliable the estimate. When added to and subtracted from the estimate, the margin of error forms the 90-percent confidence interval.

Source: U.S. Census Bureau, 2007 American Community Survey.

---

[5] This report uses the characteristics of the householder to describe the household. The householder is the person (or one of the people) in whose name the home is owned or rented and the person to whom the relationship of other household members is recorded. If a married couple owns the home jointly, either the husband or the wife may be listed as the householder. Since only one person in each household is designated as the householder, the number of householders is equal to the number of households.

[6] Because federal surveys, including the ACS, allow people to report one or more races, two ways of defining a group such as Asian are possible. The first includes those who reported Asian and no other race (Asian alone); the second includes everyone who reported Asian regardless of whether they also reported another race (Asian alone or in combination with one or more other races). The use of the single-race population in this report does not imply that it is the preferred method of presenting or analyzing data. The Census Bureau uses a variety of approaches. Some Other Race was selected by respondents who did not identify with the five Office of Management and Budget race categories.

[7] The estimates in this report (which may be shown in text, figures, and tables) are based on responses from a sample of the population and may differ from actual values because of sampling variability or other factors. As a result, apparent differences between the estimates for two or more groups may not be statistically significant. All comparative statements have undergone statistical testing and are significant at the 90-percent confidence level unless otherwise noted.

[8] The median household income of Hispanic households was not statistically different from the median household income of Some Other Race households. Because Hispanics may be any race, data for Hispanics overlap with data for racial groups.

[9] The median household income for the state of Mississippi was not statistically different from the median household income for West Virginia. The median household income for Puerto Rico was $17,741.

Table 2.
Median Household Income in the Past 12 Months by State: 2006 and 2007

(In 2007 inflation-adjusted dollars. Data are limited to the household population and exclude the population living in institutions, college dormitories, and other group quarters. For information on confidentiality protection, sampling error, nonsampling error, and definitions, see *www.census.gov/acs/www/*)

Area	2006 median household income (dollars)		2007 median household income (dollars)		Change in median income (2007 less 2006)			
					Dollars		Percent	
	Estimate	Margin of error[1] (±)	Estimate	Margin of error[1] (±)	Estimate	Margin of error[1] (±)	Estimate	Margin of error[1] (±)
United States	49,807	80	50,740	75	*933	109	*1.9	0.2
Alabama...................	39,870	500	40,554	428	*684	658	*1.7	1.6
Alaska....................	61,098	1,652	64,333	1,594	*3,235	2,295	*5.2	3.7
Arizona...................	48,622	533	49,889	508	*1,267	737	*2.6	1.5
Arkansas	37,511	602	38,134	739	623	953	1.6	2.5
California	58,277	275	59,948	295	*1,671	404	*2.8	0.7
Colorado	53,539	592	55,212	650	*1,673	879	*3.1	1.6
Connecticut	65,312	733	65,967	815	655	1,096	1.0	1.7
Delaware	54,312	1,339	54,610	1,581	298	2,072	0.5	3.8
District of Columbia	53,363	1,392	54,317	1,984	954	2,424	1.8	4.5
Florida	46,603	264	47,804	341	*1,201	431	*2.5	0.9
Georgia	48,065	471	49,136	488	*1,071	678	*2.2	1.4
Hawaii	62,926	1,283	63,746	1,923	820	2,312	1.3	3.7
Idaho	44,211	906	46,253	755	*2,042	1,179	*4.5	2.6
Illinois...................	53,444	356	54,124	370	*680	514	*1.3	1.0
Indiana...................	46,488	430	47,448	378	*960	572	*2.0	1.2
Iowa.....................	45,668	494	47,292	577	*1,624	760	*3.5	1.6
Kansas...................	46,496	524	47,451	640	*955	827	*2.0	1.8
Kentucky	40,331	441	40,267	522	−64	683	−0.2	1.7
Louisiana	40,301	473	40,926	457	625	658	1.5	1.6
Maine....................	44,646	772	45,888	710	*1,242	1,049	*2.7	2.3
Maryland	66,750	787	68,080	740	*1,330	1,081	*2.0	1.6
Massachusetts............	61,415	631	62,365	510	*950	811	*1.5	1.3
Michigan..................	48,546	371	47,950	386	*−596	535	*−1.2	1.1
Minnesota	55,527	444	55,802	605	275	750	0.5	1.3
Mississippi	35,411	613	36,338	686	*927	920	*2.6	2.6
Missouri..................	44,063	392	45,114	489	*1,051	627	*2.4	1.4
Montana..................	41,562	618	43,531	1,028	*1,969	1,200	*4.6	2.8
Nebraska.................	46,575	594	47,085	689	510	910	1.1	1.9
Nevada	54,543	946	55,062	936	519	1,331	0.9	2.4
New Hampshire	61,242	1,099	62,369	1,147	1,127	1,588	1.8	2.6
New Jersey	66,159	615	67,035	573	*876	840	*1.3	1.3
New Mexico...............	41,540	676	41,452	677	−88	957	−0.2	2.3
New York.................	52,656	330	53,514	349	*858	480	*1.6	0.9
North Carolina	43,820	462	44,670	432	*850	633	*1.9	1.4
North Dakota	43,010	1,272	43,753	1,205	743	1,752	1.7	4.0
Ohio.....................	45,664	316	46,597	304	*933	439	*2.0	1.0
Oklahoma.................	39,765	588	41,567	395	*1,802	709	*4.4	1.7
Oregon...................	47,388	600	48,730	681	*1,342	907	*2.8	1.9
Pennsylvania	47,389	311	48,576	297	*1,187	430	*2.5	0.9
Rhode Island	53,394	1,409	53,568	1,353	174	1,953	0.3	3.7
South Carolina............	41,964	459	43,329	635	*1,365	784	*3.2	1.8
South Dakota.............	43,851	1,093	43,424	944	−427	1,444	−1.0	3.3
Tennessee	41,199	449	42,367	345	*1,168	566	*2.8	1.4
Texas....................	46,013	269	47,548	308	*1,535	409	*3.3	0.9
Utah.....................	52,636	726	55,109	762	*2,473	1,052	*4.6	2.0
Vermont..................	49,090	1,207	49,907	1,176	817	1,685	1.7	3.4
Virginia...................	57,869	492	59,562	589	*1,693	767	*2.9	1.3
Washington	54,149	460	55,591	501	*1,442	680	*2.6	1.2
West Virginia	36,006	607	37,060	760	*1,054	972	*2.9	2.7
Wisconsin.................	50,052	381	50,578	364	526	527	1.0	1.0
Wyoming	49,006	1,484	51,731	1,322	*2,725	1,988	*5.4	3.9
Puerto Rico	18,184	386	17,741	390	−443	549	−2.5	3.1

* Statistically different from zero at the 90-percent confidence level.

[1] Data are based on a sample and are subject to sampling variability. A margin of error is a measure of an estimate's variability. The larger the margin of error in relation to the size of the estimate, the less reliable the estimate. When added to and subtracted from the estimate, the margin of error forms the 90-percent confidence interval.

Source: U.S. Census Bureau, 2006 and 2007 American Community Surveys, and 2006 and 2007 Puerto Rico Community Surveys.

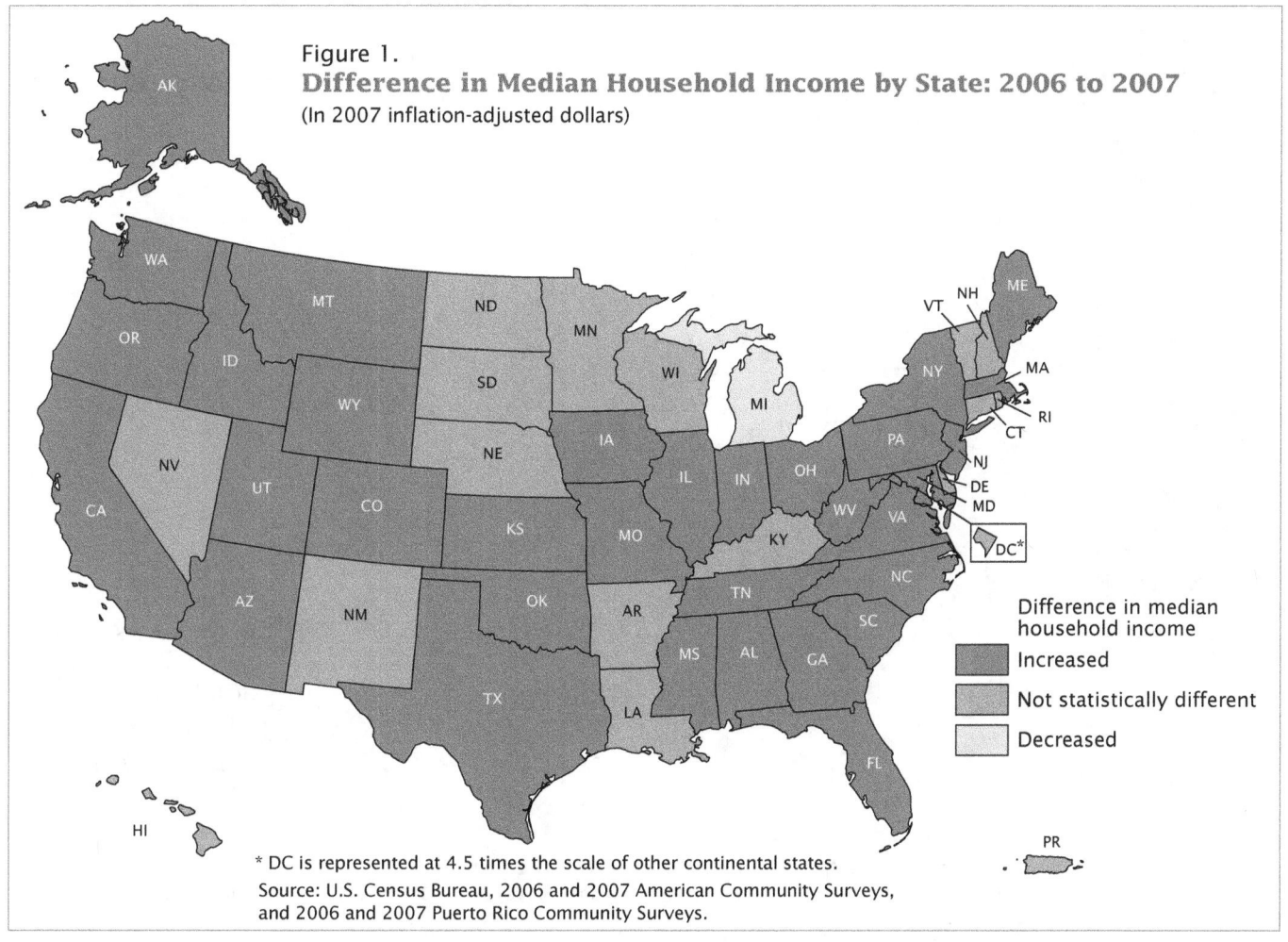

Figure 1.
Difference in Median Household Income by State: 2006 to 2007
(In 2007 inflation-adjusted dollars)

Difference in median
household income

Increased

Not statistically different

Decreased

* DC is represented at 4.5 times the scale of other continental states.
Source: U.S. Census Bureau, 2006 and 2007 American Community Surveys,
and 2006 and 2007 Puerto Rico Community Surveys.

Table 2 and Figure 1 show that real median household income rose between the 2006 ACS and the 2007 ACS in 33 states, while one state—Michigan—experienced a decline.[10] (All year-to-year comparisons using ACS data should be viewed with caution. See footnote 3 for more information.) For the states that experienced increases, ten states were in the West (Alaska, Arizona, California, Colorado, Idaho, Montana, Oregon, Utah, Washington, and Wyoming), twelve states were in the South

(Alabama, Florida, Georgia, Maryland, Mississippi, North Carolina, Oklahoma, South Carolina, Tennessee, Texas, Virginia, and West Virginia), six states were in the Midwest (Iowa, Illinois, Indiana, Kansas, Missouri, and Ohio), and five states were in the Northeast (Maine, Massachusetts, New Jersey, New York, and Pennsylvania).[11]

Figure 2 displays the relationships of state median household incomes to the median for the United States. Median incomes in 18 states and the District of Columbia were above the U.S. median, while 29 state medians were below it. Three states had median household incomes that were not statistically different from the U.S. median.

The states in the Northeast tended to have median incomes above the U.S. median. Six of the nine Northeast states—Connecticut, Massachusetts, New Hampshire, New Jersey, New York, and Rhode Island—had median household incomes above the U.S. median, while Maine and Pennsylvania were below the U.S. median. Vermont's median household income was not statistically different from the U.S. median.

---

[10] All income values are adjusted to reflect 2007 dollars. "Real" refers to income after adjusting for inflation. The adjustment is based on percentage changes in prices between 2006 and 2007 and is computed by dividing the annual average Consumer Price Index Research Series (CPI-U-RS) for 2007 by the annual average for 2006. The CPI-U-RS values for 1947 to 2007 are available on the Internet at <www.census.gov/hhes/www /income/income07/cpiurs.html>. Inflation between 2006 and 2007 was 2.8 percent.

[11] The Northeast region includes the states of Connecticut, Maine, Massachusetts, New Hampshire, New Jersey, New York, Pennsylvania, Rhode Island, and Vermont. The Midwest region includes the states of Illinois, Indiana, Iowa, Kansas, Michigan, Minnesota, Missouri, Nebraska, North Dakota, Ohio, South Dakota, and Wisconsin. The South region includes the states of Alabama, Arkansas, Delaware, Florida, Georgia, Kentucky, Louisiana, Maryland, Mississippi, North Carolina, Oklahoma, South Carolina, Tennessee, Texas, Virginia, West Virginia, and the District of Columbia, a state equivalent. The West region includes the states of Alaska, Arizona, California, Colorado, Hawaii, Idaho, Montana, Nevada, New Mexico, Oregon, Utah, Washington, and Wyoming.

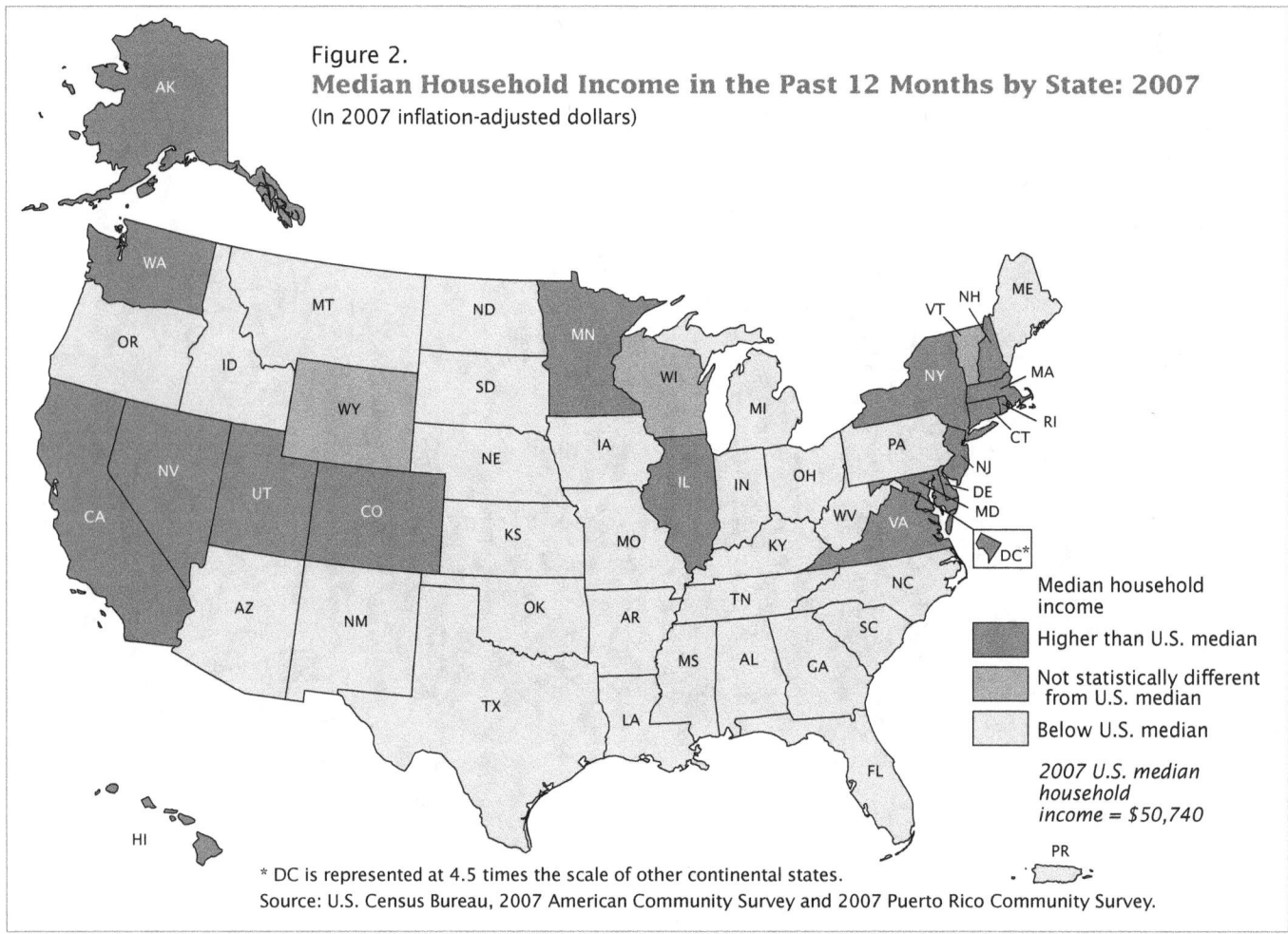

Figure 2.
Median Household Income in the Past 12 Months by State: 2007
(In 2007 inflation-adjusted dollars)

Median household income

Higher than U.S. median

Not statistically different from U.S. median

Below U.S. median

2007 U.S. median household income = $50,740

* DC is represented at 4.5 times the scale of other continental states.
Source: U.S. Census Bureau, 2007 American Community Survey and 2007 Puerto Rico Community Survey.

Similarly, states in the West were likely to be above the U.S. median, with 7 of the 13 states having household incomes above the U.S. median. They were Alaska, California, Colorado, Hawaii, Nevada, Utah, and Washington. Those below the U.S. median in the West were Arizona, Idaho, Montana, New Mexico, and Oregon. Wyoming had a median household income that was not statistically different from the U.S. median.

The majority of states in the Midwest (9 out of 12) and the South (13 out of 17) had median incomes that were below the U.S. median. Illinois and Minnesota in the Midwest and Delaware, Maryland, Virginia, and the District of Columbia in the South had incomes above the national median. Wisconsin, in the Midwest, had a median income that was not

statistically different from the U.S. median.

Incomes were generally higher on the East and West coasts than they were in the rest of the country in the 2007 ACS. Figure 2 shows that 13 out of the 18 states with median household incomes higher than the U.S. median were East and West coast states. Of the 5 states bordering the Pacific Ocean—Alaska, California, Hawaii, Oregon, and Washington—only Oregon had a median income that was lower than the U.S. median. Of the 14 states bordering the Atlantic Ocean, 9 had medians above the U.S. median.

In the 2007 ACS, the total U.S. median household income in metropolitan or micropolitan statistical areas was $51,658 (see Appendix Table A-1). For households in principal cities within metropolitan

statistical areas, the median was $45,590; for households in principal cities within micropolitan statistical areas, the median was $35,962; and for households not in metropolitan or micropolitan statistical areas, the median was $37,844. Among the states, while not statistically different from Alaska and New Jersey, Maryland had the highest median household income in metropolitan or micropolitan statistical areas ($68,512), and Mississippi, while not statistically different from West Virginia, had the lowest at $38,380. Median incomes were lower for households in principal cities of metropolitan statistical areas than households not in principal cities in all states except Alaska, where they were not statistically different.[12]

---

[12] The District of Columbia, Massachusetts, New Jersey, and Rhode Island do not contain any micropolitan statistical areas.

Median Household Income for Counties and Places

One of the strengths of the ACS is its ability to produce estimates for substate geographic areas. Because smaller geographic areas differ from larger ones in many ways, this report divides counties and places into two groups—those with populations of 250,000 or more (larger areas) and those with populations from 65,000 to 249,999 (smaller areas).[13] Table 3 identifies some of the larger counties and places that have high and low median

[13] Population size is based on the 2007 population estimates released as part of the Census Bureau's Population Estimates Program.

household incomes, while Table 4 does the same for smaller counties and places.[14]

Median Income in Larger Areas

For counties with 250,000 or more people, median household income estimates ranged from $107,207 for Loudoun County, VA, to $29,347 for Cameron County, TX.[15] For places

[14] Because of sampling error, the estimates for the high- and low-income counties and places shown in Tables 3 and 4 may not be statistically different from one another or from counties and places not shown.

[15] For the discussion of the ten highest and lowest income counties and in the release of county-level data, parishes in Louisiana and incorporated cities in several states are treated as county equivalents. The median household income for Loudoun County, VA, is not statis-

with 250,000 people or more, median household incomes ranged from $84,492 for Plano city, TX, to $28,097 for Detroit city, MI.[16]

All of the counties in Table 3 with high median household income estimates are found in states with incomes above the U.S. median. Eight of the ten counties in Table 3 with lower incomes are in states

tically different from the median household income for Fairfax County, VA. The median household income for Cameron County, TX, is not statistically different from the median household income for Hidalgo County, TX.

[16] The median household income for Detroit city, MI, is not statistically different from the median household income for Miami city, FL; Buffalo city, NY; or Cleveland city, OH, nor is it statistically different from the median household income for Cameron County, TX.

Table 3.
Median Household Income in the Past 12 Months for Ten of the Highest and Lowest Income Counties and Places With 250,000 or More People: 2007

(In 2007 inflation-adjusted dollars. Data are limited to the household population and exclude the population living in institutions, college dormitories, and other group quarters. For information on confidentiality protection, sampling error, nonsampling error, and definitions, see www.census.gov/acs/www/)

Area	Ten of the highest median incomes (dollars)		Area	Ten of the lowest median incomes (dollars)	
	Estimate	Margin of error[1](±)		Estimate	Margin of error[1](±)
Counties[2]			Counties[2]		
Loudoun County, VA	107,207	3,203	Marion County, FL	39,294	2,037
Fairfax County, VA	105,241	1,822	Mobile County, AL	37,391	1,544
Howard County, MD	101,672	3,594	Baltimore city, MD	36,949	896
Somerset County, NJ	97,658	4,270	Philadelphia County, PA	35,365	870
Morris County, NJ	94,684	2,695	El Paso County, TX	34,980	1,479
Douglas County, CO	92,824	2,752	Caddo Parish, LA	34,744	2,383
Montgomery County, MD	91,835	2,126	St. Louis city, MO	34,191	1,789
Nassau County, NY	89,782	1,987	Bronx County, NY	34,156	1,138
Prince William County, VA	87,243	3,644	Hidalgo County, TX	30,295	1,711
Santa Clara County, CA	84,360	1,608	Cameron County, TX	29,347	1,701
Places[2]			Places[2]		
Plano city, TX	84,492	4,929	Toledo city, OH	35,216	1,866
San Jose city, CA	76,963	2,580	Memphis city, TN	35,143	1,238
Anchorage municipality, AK	68,726	3,329	Newark city, NJ	34,452	1,922
San Francisco city, CA	68,023	3,283	St. Louis city, MO	34,191	1,789
San Diego city, CA	61,863	1,332	Cincinnati city, OH	33,006	1,678
Virginia Beach city, VA	61,462	1,699	Pittsburgh city, PA	32,363	1,394
Seattle city, WA	57,849	2,274	Buffalo city, NY	29,706	1,544
Anaheim city, CA	57,059	2,623	Miami city, FL	29,075	1,916
Riverside city, CA	55,999	2,860	Cleveland city, OH	28,512	1,654
Honolulu CDP, HI	55,536	2,737	Detroit city, MI	28,097	1,138

[1] Data are based on a sample and are subject to sampling variability. A margin of error is a measure of an estimate's variability. The larger the margin of error in relation to the size of the estimate, the less reliable the estimate. When added to and subtracted from the estimate, the margin of error forms the 90-percent confidence interval.
[2] Population size is based on the 2007 population estimates released as part of the U.S. Census Bureau's Population Estimates Program.

Note: Because of sampling variability, some of the estimates in this table may not be statistically different from one another or from estimates for other geographic areas not listed in the table.

Source: U.S. Census Bureau, 2007 American Community Survey.

Table 4.
Median Household Income in the Past 12 Months for Ten of the Highest and Lowest Income Counties and Places With 65,000 to 249,999 People: 2007

(In 2007 inflation-adjusted dollars. Data are limited to the household population and exclude the population living in institutions, college dormitories, and other group quarters. For information on confidentiality protection, sampling error, nonsampling error, and definitions, see *www.census.gov/acs/www/*)

Area	Ten of the highest median incomes (dollars)		Area	Ten of the lowest median incomes (dollars)	
	Estimate	Margin of error[1](±)		Estimate	Margin of error[1](±)
Counties[2]			Counties[2]		
Hunterdon County, NJ	100,327	4,282	Imperial County, CA	31,912	2,685
Calvert County, MD............	95,134	8,091	Orangeburg County, SC.......	31,877	3,948
Arlington County, VA...........	94,876	4,154	Potter County, TX	31,788	2,250
Stafford County, VA...........	87,629	5,720	Cabell County, WV	31,592	2,915
Fauquier County, VA...........	84,888	13,752	Scioto County, OH	31,446	3,987
Forsyth County, GA...........	84,872	4,067	Fayette County, PA	31,344	1,888
Putnam County, NY	84,624	3,803	Lauderdale County, MS	31,054	2,331
Marin County, CA	83,870	4,851	Robeson County, NC	30,882	1,569
Charles County, MD	83,412	4,582	Apache County, AZ	30,534	4,004
Carroll County, MD	82,492	5,651	St. Landry Parish, LA	26,275	2,777
Places[2]			Places[2]		
Pleasanton city, CA...........	113,345	8,196	Passaic city, NJ	27,691	5,937
Newton city, MA..............	110,885	10,361	Hartford city, CT	27,654	2,780
Newport Beach city, CA	110,511	5,967	Gainesville city, FL...........	27,479	3,523
Yorba Linda city, CA	109,681	7,142	Gary city, IN	26,725	2,438
Flower Mound town, TX	105,812	6,366	Macon city, GA	26,555	4,065
Highlands Ranch CDP, CO	99,066	5,052	Flint city, MI.................	26,143	1,869
Irvine city, CA	98,923	4,821	Reading city, PA	25,536	2,141
West Bloomfield Township CDP, MI..................	98,832	8,442	Camden city, NJ .... Bloomington city, IN...........	25,389 25,225	2,435 3,939
Chino Hills city, CA...........	96,733	8,745	Youngstown city, OH..........	24,941	2,349
Naperville city, IL.............	96,548	4,752			

[1] Data are based on a sample and are subject to sampling variability. A margin of error is a measure of an estimate's variability. The larger the margin of error in relation to the size of the estimate, the less reliable the estimate. When added to and subtracted from the estimate, the margin of error forms the 90-percent confidence interval.
[2] Population size is based on the 2007 population estimates released as part of the U.S. Census Bureau's Population Estimates Program.

Note: Because of sampling variability, some of the estimates in this table may not be statistically different from one another or from estimates for other geographic areas not listed in the table.

Source: U.S. Census Bureau, 2007 American Community Survey.

with median household incomes below the U.S. median. The two exceptions are Bronx County, NY, and Baltimore city, MD. Both Maryland and New York have counties (or county equivalents) on both the high and the low median household income lists. Median household incomes in the state of Maryland for larger counties ranged from $101,672 for Howard County to $36,949 for Baltimore city, while in the state of New York, incomes ranged from $89,782 for Nassau County to $34,156 for Bronx County.

Unlike the county ranking, one of the ten places with a high median income—Plano city, TX—is not in a state with a median household income above the U.S. median. Eight of the ten lower-income large places are in lower-income states. The two exceptions are Newark city, NJ, and Buffalo city, NY, which are both in states with median incomes above the U.S. level.

Median Income in Smaller Areas

Table 4 lists smaller counties and places with both high and low median incomes. For counties with 65,000 to 249,999 people, median household incomes ranged from $100,327 for Hunterdon County, NJ, to $26,275 for St. Landry Parish,

LA.[17] Median household incomes for places with 65,000 to 249,999 people ranged from $113,345 for Pleasanton city, CA, to $24,941 for Youngstown city, OH.[18]

---

[17] The median household income for Hunterdon County, NJ, is not statistically different from the median household income for Calvert County, MD, or Arlington County, VA. The median household income for St. Landry Parish, LA, is not statistically different from the median household income for Apache County, AZ.

[18] The median household income for Pleasanton city, CA, is not statistically different from the median household income for Newton city, MA; Newport Beach city, CA; Yorba Linda city, CA; or Flower Mound town, TX. The median household income for Youngstown city, OH, is not statistically different from any of the ten lowest-income places with 65,000 people to 249,999 people in Table 4, nor is it statistically different from the median household income for St. Landry Parish, LA.

Nine of the ten counties with high median household incomes are found in states with median incomes above the U.S. median; the exception is Forsyth County, GA. Nine of the ten counties with lower incomes in Table 4 are in states with incomes below the U.S. median; the exception is Imperial County, CA. California has counties on both the high and the low median household income lists. Median household incomes for smaller counties in California ranged from $83,870 for Marin County to $31,912 for Imperial County.

Eight of the ten places with high median household incomes are in states with median incomes above the U.S. median; the exceptions are Flower Mound town, TX, and West Bloomfield Township CDP, MI. At the place level, seven of the ten lower-income places are in lower income states. The exceptions are Passaic city, NJ; Hartford city, CT; and Camden city, NJ, which are in states with medians above the U.S. level. Michigan had smaller places on both the high and the low lists. Median household incomes for smaller places in Michigan ranged from $98,832 for West Bloomfield Township CDP to $26,143 for Flint city.[19]

19 The median household income for Flint city, MI, is not statistically different from the median household incomes for Pontiac city, MI, and Kalamazoo, MI.

Income Inequality for the United States and the States

This section focuses on two widely used measures of income inequality —the Gini index and shares of aggregate household income by quintile. These estimates were calculated for the first time in the 2006 ACS. The definitions of these measures and their calculation methods are discussed in the text box "What Are Shares of Aggregate Household Income and a Gini Index?" National estimates of these measures are also calculated using CPS ASEC data, and they are included in the publication *Income, Poverty, and Health Insurance Coverage in the United States: 2007*, along with historical data.

The Gini index in the 2007 ACS was .467 for the United States. As shown in Table 5, the Gini index varied by state, ranging from .542 for the District of Columbia to .409 for both Utah and Alaska.[20] Figure 3 displays the relationship of state Gini indexes to the Gini index for the United States. Five states and the District of Columbia showed more income inequality (a higher Gini index) than the nation, while 33 states showed less income inequality (a lower Gini index).

20 The Gini index for the District of Columbia is not statistically different from the Gini index for Puerto Rico. The Gini indexes for Utah and Alaska are not statistically different from the Gini index for New Hampshire, and the Gini index for Alaska is also not statistically different from the Gini indexes for Hawaii and South Dakota.

What Are Shares of Aggregate Household Income and a Gini Index?

Income inequality measures look at how income is being distributed across a population. Two of the most widely used measures of income inequality are the shares of aggregate household income by quintile and the Gini index. This report presents these two measures for the household population.

The share of aggregate income by quintile is the amount of aggregate income that households within each fifth of the income distribution receive as a percentage of overall aggregate income of all households. The Gini index is a summary measure of income inequality. It indicates how much the income distribution differs from a proportionate distribution (one where everyone would have the same income; for example, 20 percent of the population would hold 20 percent of the income, 40 percent of the population would hold 40 percent of the income, etc.). The Gini index varies from 0 to 1, where 0 indicates perfect equality (a proportional distribution of income), and 1 indicates perfect inequality (where one person has all the income and no one else has any).

For more information on income inequality measures, see Current Population Reports, P60-204, *The Changing Shape of the Nation's Income Distribution: 1947–1998*.

Table 5.
Gini Coefficients and Shares of Income by Quintile in the Past 12 Months by State: 2007

(Data are limited to the household population and exclude the population living in institutions, college dormitories, and other group quarters. For information on confidentiality protection, sampling error, nonsampling error, and definitions, see *www.census.gov/acs/www/*)

| Area | Gini coefficients | | Shares of income by quintile | | | | | | | | | |
| | | | Lowest quintile | | Second quintile | | Third quintile | | Fourth quintile | | Highest quintile | |
	Esti-mate	Margin of error[1] (±)	Esti-mate	Margin of error[1] (±)	Esti-mate	Margin of error[1] (±)	Esti-mate	Margin of error[1] (±)	Esti-mate	Margin of error[1] (±)	Esti-mate	Margin of error[1] (±)
United States	0.467	0.0001	3.4	0.01	8.8	0.01	14.7	0.01	22.8	0.01	50.3	0.09
Alabama	0.471	0.0050	3.2	0.22	8.5	0.19	14.7	0.19	23.4	0.27	50.2	0.47
Alaska	0.409	0.0125	4.2	0.20	10.5	0.34	16.4	0.43	24.0	0.60	44.9	1.19
Arizona	0.448	0.0044	3.8	0.17	9.4	0.21	15.1	0.13	23.1	0.23	48.7	0.41
Arkansas	0.462	0.0069	3.5	0.13	8.8	0.19	14.8	0.25	23.2	0.32	49.7	0.64
California	0.469	0.0026	3.4	0.01	8.7	0.04	14.6	0.05	22.8	0.16	50.5	0.20
Colorado	0.452	0.0055	3.8	0.18	9.3	0.17	15.2	0.20	23.1	0.24	48.9	0.52
Connecticut	0.481	0.0052	3.3	0.20	8.7	0.18	14.3	0.19	21.8	0.28	51.9	0.54
Delaware	0.435	0.0103	3.8	0.28	9.7	0.29	15.6	0.37	23.7	0.39	47.3	0.95
District of Columbia	0.542	0.0129	2.1	0.25	6.8	0.36	12.5	0.42	21.6	0.61	56.9	1.26
Florida	0.469	0.0033	3.7	0.14	8.9	0.16	14.4	0.23	22.2	0.21	50.8	0.32
Georgia	0.464	0.0036	3.4	0.01	9.0	0.07	14.8	0.17	22.8	0.19	50.0	0.36
Hawaii	0.422	0.0093	3.9	0.22	10.2	0.32	16.1	0.33	23.7	0.39	46.1	0.86
Idaho	0.436	0.0100	4.3	0.20	9.8	0.25	15.3	0.35	22.6	0.38	48.1	0.93
Illinois	0.466	0.0033	3.4	0.01	8.9	0.13	14.9	0.21	22.7	0.15	50.1	0.33
Indiana	0.429	0.0042	4.0	0.16	9.9	0.12	15.8	0.16	23.5	0.21	46.8	0.37
Iowa	0.426	0.0056	4.1	0.11	9.8	0.20	15.9	0.23	23.6	0.26	46.6	0.55
Kansas	0.444	0.0064	4.0	0.19	9.4	0.26	15.1	0.26	23.1	0.25	48.4	0.60
Kentucky	0.465	0.0057	3.3	0.07	8.6	0.20	14.9	0.20	23.5	0.28	49.7	0.55
Louisiana	0.478	0.0044	3.0	0.16	8.2	0.16	14.5	0.22	23.5	0.26	50.7	0.47
Maine	0.440	0.0094	3.9	0.18	9.5	0.24	15.5	0.30	23.2	0.38	47.8	0.87
Maryland	0.442	0.0043	3.7	0.13	9.5	0.21	15.5	0.22	23.2	0.25	48.0	0.39
Massachusetts	0.467	0.0043	3.1	0.10	8.7	0.16	15.1	0.17	23.2	0.17	49.9	0.41
Michigan	0.448	0.0027	3.6	0.15	9.2	0.07	15.3	0.11	23.6	0.19	48.4	0.31
Minnesota	0.436	0.0042	3.9	0.12	9.8	0.16	15.6	0.12	23.1	0.19	47.6	0.35
Mississippi	0.480	0.0065	3.2	0.16	8.2	0.22	14.3	0.25	23.2	0.28	51.2	0.64
Missouri	0.450	0.0047	3.7	0.18	9.2	0.16	15.2	0.24	23.2	0.21	48.7	0.43
Montana	0.443	0.0104	3.8	0.28	9.4	0.30	15.5	0.35	23.3	0.49	48.0	0.96
Nebraska	0.429	0.0055	4.1	0.15	9.8	0.17	15.7	0.25	23.5	0.29	46.9	0.54
Nevada	0.437	0.0070	4.2	0.17	9.9	0.21	15.2	0.28	22.5	0.32	48.1	0.65
New Hampshire	0.417	0.0080	4.3	0.24	10.2	0.24	16.1	0.28	23.5	0.36	45.9	0.73
New Jersey	0.464	0.0033	3.3	0.17	8.9	0.21	14.9	0.19	22.9	0.20	49.9	0.36
New Mexico	0.459	0.0077	3.4	0.20	8.9	0.27	14.9	0.31	23.5	0.35	49.3	0.75
New York	0.500	0.0031	2.9	0.01	8.0	0.07	13.9	0.21	22.1	0.17	53.2	0.29
North Carolina	0.465	0.0032	3.4	0.04	8.8	0.18	14.8	0.12	22.9	0.15	50.1	0.33
North Dakota	0.440	0.0122	3.8	0.24	9.3	0.34	15.7	0.43	23.7	0.48	47.6	1.13
Ohio	0.448	0.0032	3.5	0.23	9.3	0.06	15.4	0.14	23.4	0.12	48.4	0.31
Oklahoma	0.463	0.0058	3.5	0.07	8.9	0.20	14.8	0.20	23.0	0.28	49.8	0.56
Oregon	0.442	0.0049	3.8	0.06	9.5	0.18	15.4	0.23	23.3	0.24	48.0	0.49
Pennsylvania	0.460	0.0033	3.6	0.17	8.9	0.19	14.9	0.18	23.0	0.18	49.6	0.29
Rhode Island	0.457	0.0089	3.2	0.19	8.8	0.31	15.4	0.32	24.0	0.41	48.7	0.86
South Carolina	0.459	0.0051	3.4	0.22	9.0	0.13	15.0	0.24	23.4	0.25	49.2	0.48
South Dakota	0.423	0.0085	4.2	0.24	10.0	0.29	15.8	0.26	23.4	0.38	46.6	0.77
Tennessee	0.471	0.0041	3.4	0.08	8.8	0.15	14.7	0.21	22.5	0.23	50.7	0.39
Texas	0.473	0.0024	3.3	0.20	8.6	0.04	14.4	0.04	22.8	0.18	50.9	0.25
Utah	0.409	0.0067	4.6	0.16	10.6	0.21	16.0	0.24	23.1	0.28	45.7	0.60
Vermont	0.428	0.0095	4.1	0.21	9.9	0.28	15.7	0.37	23.3	0.42	46.9	0.92
Virginia	0.456	0.0037	3.5	0.10	9.1	0.17	15.0	0.20	23.0	0.19	49.4	0.38
Washington	0.444	0.0044	3.8	0.17	9.5	0.15	15.4	0.19	23.2	0.21	48.2	0.40
West Virginia	0.454	0.0075	3.5	0.16	8.8	0.24	15.1	0.28	24.0	0.36	48.6	0.73
Wisconsin	0.428	0.0040	4.1	0.10	9.9	0.16	15.9	0.23	23.4	0.18	46.8	0.38
Wyoming	0.437	0.0223	4.2	0.31	9.6	0.47	15.4	0.67	23.0	0.94	47.7	2.09
Puerto Rico	0.544	0.0061	1.5	0.09	6.6	0.18	12.8	0.25	22.8	0.32	56.2	0.66

[1] Data are based on a sample and are subject to sampling variability. A margin of error is a measure of an estimate's variability. The larger the margin of error in relation to the size of the estimate, the less reliable the estimate. When added to and subtracted from the estimate, the margin of error forms the 90-percent confidence interval.

Source: U.S. Census Bureau, 2007 American Community Survey and 2007 Puerto Rico Community Survey.

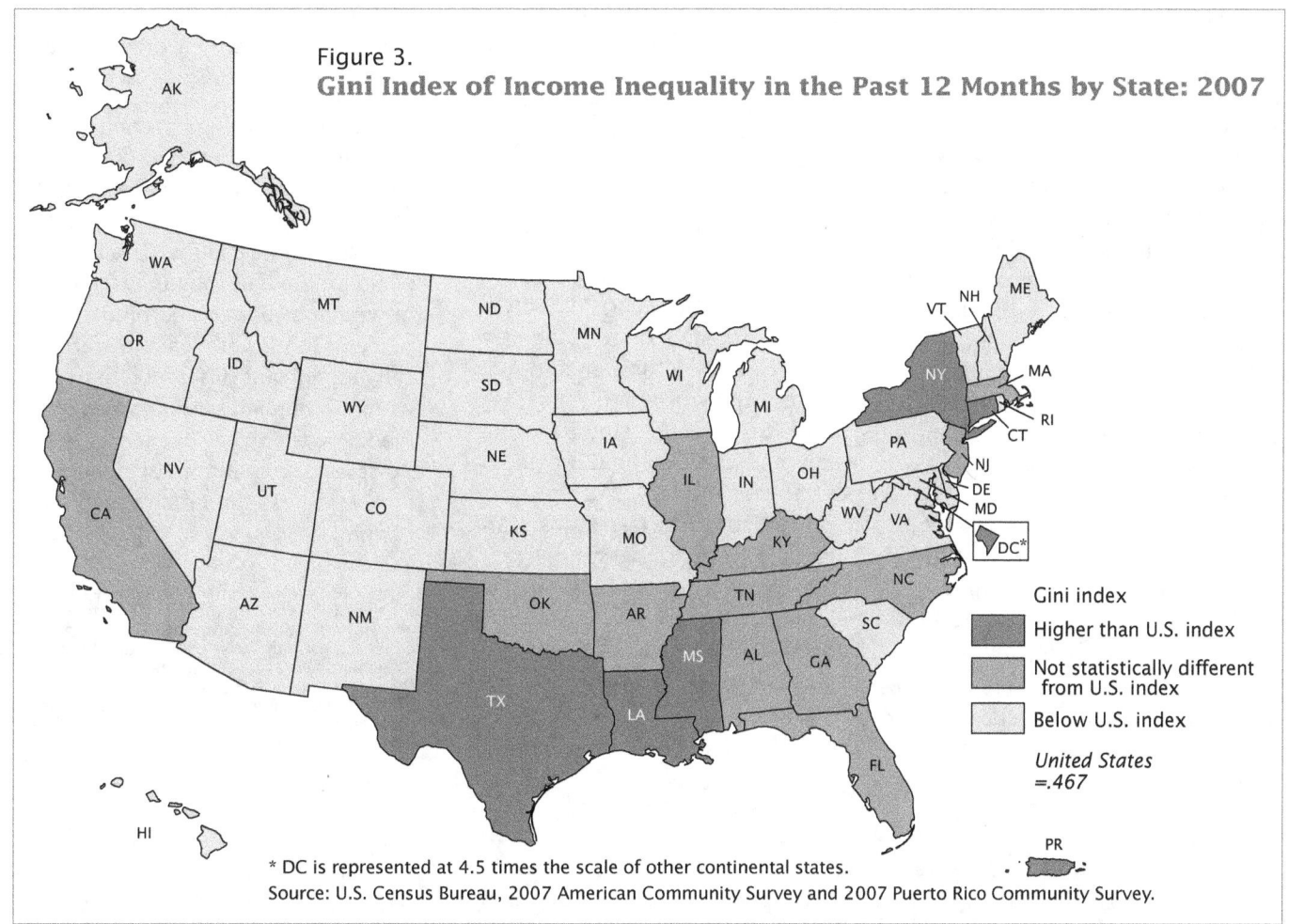

Figure 3.
Gini Index of Income Inequality in the Past 12 Months by State: 2007

Gini index

- Higher than U.S. index
- Not statistically different from U.S. index
- Below U.S. index

United States = .467

* DC is represented at 4.5 times the scale of other continental states.
Source: U.S. Census Bureau, 2007 American Community Survey and 2007 Puerto Rico Community Survey.

Twelve states had Gini indexes that were not statistically different from the national estimate.

Also included in Table 5 are shares of aggregate income by quintile for the United States, states, and the District of Columbia. The shares of aggregate income held by the lowest quintile of households ranged from 4.6 percent for Utah to 2.1 percent for the District of Columbia. The shares of aggregate income held by the highest quintile of households ranged from 56.9 percent for the District of Columbia to 44.9 percent for Alaska.[21]

---

[21] The share of aggregate income for the highest quintile for Alaska was not statistically different from the shares of aggregate income for the highest quintile for Hawaii, New Hampshire, and Utah.

EARNINGS OF MEN AND WOMEN

This section examines the earnings of men and women by geography, race and Hispanic origin, educational attainment, industry and occupation, and class of worker. Median earnings are calculated only for people 16 years and older with earnings. The tables and figures focus on various aspects of earnings. Table 6 presents earnings by state for full-time, year-round workers. Table 7 includes earnings by race and Hispanic origin for full-time, year-round workers; earnings by educational attainment for people 25 years and older (regardless of hours and weeks worked); and earnings by type of industry and class of worker for full-time, year-round civilian workers. Table 8 includes earnings by occupation for full-time, year-round civilian workers. For most individuals, earnings are the largest component of their total income. The text box "What Are 'Earnings'?" describes this income category.

Men's and Women's Earnings by State

Table 6 shows earnings data by state and the District of Columbia in the 2007 ACS for men and women who worked full-time, year-round. Some of the states that had high median household incomes, as shown in Table 2, such as Connecticut, New Jersey, Maryland, Massachusetts, New Hampshire, and Alaska, also had high median earnings for men, that is, earnings above $50,000. No state had median earnings for women above $50,000, but in the District of Columbia, Maryland, New Jersey, Massachusetts, and Connecticut, median earnings for women were above $40,000.

The median earnings of men in the United States in the 2007 ACS were $44,255; for women median earnings were $34,278, or 77.5 percent of men's earnings. The District of Columbia had the highest ratio of women's-to-men's earnings (93.4 percent), and there was no statistically significant difference between women's median earnings and men's median earnings.[22] In each of the 50 states, women's median earnings were less than men's median earnings.

---

[22] The ratio of women's to men's earnings for the District of Columbia and Puerto Rico was not statistically different from 100 percent. The median earnings for men in Puerto Rico were $20,242, and the median earnings for women were $19,812. The median earnings for men in Puerto Rico were not statistically different from the median earnings for women in Puerto Rico.

What Are "Earnings"?

"Earnings" are the sum of wage and salary income and self-employment income. Earnings are often the largest part of overall income. The 2007 ACS showed that 81 percent of aggregate household income came from earnings.

This report presents information on year-round, full-time workers 16 years or older, unless noted otherwise. "Year-round" means an individual worked 50 or more weeks in the past 12 months, including paid time off for sick leave or vacation. "Full-time" means that the individual usually worked 35 or more hours per week.

The text of the two 2007 ACS questions used to determine earnings is:

41. INCOME IN THE PAST 12 MONTHS.

Mark (X) the "Yes" box for each type of income this person received, and give your best estimate of the TOTAL AMOUNT during the PAST 12 MONTHS. (NOTE: The "past 12 months" is the period from today's date one year ago through today.)

Mark (X) the "No" box to show types of income NOT received.

If net income was a loss, mark the "Loss" box to the right of the dollar amount.

For income received jointly, report the appropriate share for each person—or, if that's not possible, report the whole income for only one person and mark the "No" box for the other person.

a. Wages, salary, commissions, bonuses, or tips from all jobs. *Report amount before deductions for taxes, bonds, dues, or other items.*

b. Self-employment income from own nonfarm businesses or farm businesses, including proprietorships and partnerships. *Report NET income after business expenses.*

ACS questionnaires can be found at <www.census.gov/acs/www/SBasics/SQuest/SQuest1.htm>.

Table 6.
Median Earnings in the Past 12 Months of Full-Time, Year-Round Workers 16 and Older by Sex and Women's Earnings as a Percentage of Men's Earnings by State: 2007

(In 2007 inflation-adjusted dollars. For information on confidentiality protection, sampling error, nonsampling error, and definitions, see www.census.gov/acs/www/)

| Area | Median earnings (dollars) | | | | Women's earnings as a percentage of men's earnings | |
| | Men | | Women | | | |
	Estimate	Margin of error[1] (±)	Estimate	Margin of error[1] (±)	Estimate	Margin of error[1] (±)
United States.............	44,255	147	34,278	85	77.5	0.3
Alabama	40,829	370	29,756	572	72.9	1.5
Alaska.......................	51,275	873	37,835	1,913	73.8	3.9
Arizona	41,308	346	33,723	765	81.6	2.0
Arkansas.....................	36,379	449	26,815	522	73.7	1.7
California.....................	46,404	256	38,903	353	83.8	0.9
Colorado	46,230	574	36,827	468	79.7	1.4
Connecticut	55,394	904	41,868	514	75.6	1.5
Delaware.....................	47,964	1,879	38,543	1,501	80.4	4.4
District of Columbia...........	52,860	4,534	49,364	2,451	93.4	9.3
Florida.......................	40,238	206	32,150	195	79.9	0.6
Georgia	41,837	269	33,351	557	79.7	1.4
Hawaii.......................	44,802	1,552	35,471	780	79.2	3.2
Idaho........................	39,413	1,046	28,846	835	73.2	2.9
Illinois.......................	48,562	549	35,638	324	73.4	1.1
Indiana.......................	43,410	586	31,158	263	71.8	1.1
Iowa.........................	41,375	294	30,925	299	74.7	0.9
Kansas	42,041	417	31,145	387	74.1	1.2
Kentucky	39,920	713	29,957	402	75.0	1.7
Louisiana.....................	41,980	423	27,469	623	65.4	1.6
Maine........................	41,704	549	31,496	551	75.5	1.7
Maryland	54,501	976	44,022	716	80.8	2.0
Massachusetts................	53,602	822	42,062	355	78.5	1.4
Michigan	48,512	609	34,849	411	71.8	1.2
Minnesota	47,602	607	36,707	343	77.1	1.2
Mississippi...................	36,819	616	26,838	512	72.9	1.8
Missouri......................	41,347	365	30,827	289	74.6	1.0
Montana	38,230	1,568	26,598	635	69.6	3.3
Nebraska.....................	39,070	864	30,406	512	77.8	2.2
Nevada	42,787	1,176	34,164	809	79.8	2.9
New Hampshire................	51,385	525	35,722	694	69.5	1.5
New Jersey	54,846	772	42,221	395	77.0	1.3
New Mexico...................	38,366	1,312	30,188	573	78.7	3.1
New York.....................	47,198	346	38,830	438	82.3	1.1
North Carolina................	39,447	675	31,738	245	80.5	1.5
North Dakota..................	40,028	1,158	27,554	753	68.8	2.7
Ohio.........................	44,443	430	32,853	372	73.9	1.1
Oklahoma	37,884	907	29,378	580	77.5	2.4
Oregon	42,389	598	32,538	679	76.8	1.9
Pennsylvania..................	44,755	411	33,438	343	74.7	1.0
Rhode Island..................	48,492	1,983	37,475	1,231	77.3	4.1
South Carolina................	40,139	397	30,124	362	75.0	1.2
South Dakota..................	36,726	799	26,965	646	73.4	2.4
Tennessee....................	39,207	606	30,178	264	77.0	1.4
Texas........................	40,344	215	31,845	205	78.9	0.7
Utah.........................	43,035	926	31,001	467	72.0	1.9
Vermont......................	40,834	712	34,341	1,091	84.1	3.0
Virginia	48,142	779	36,971	435	76.8	1.5
Washington	50,269	375	37,454	527	74.5	1.2
West Virginia..................	40,126	829	26,719	538	66.6	1.9
Wisconsin	44,105	583	32,265	247	73.2	1.1
Wyoming	45,310	1,711	28,540	1,967	63.0	5.0
Puerto Rico	20,242	461	19,812	414	97.9	3.0

[1] Data are based on a sample and are subject to sampling variability. A margin of error is a measure of an estimate's variability. The larger the margin of error in relation to the size of the estimate, the less reliable the estimate. When added to and subtracted from the estimate, the margin of error forms the 90-percent confidence interval.

Source: U.S. Census Bureau, 2007 American Community Survey and 2007 Puerto Rico Community Survey.

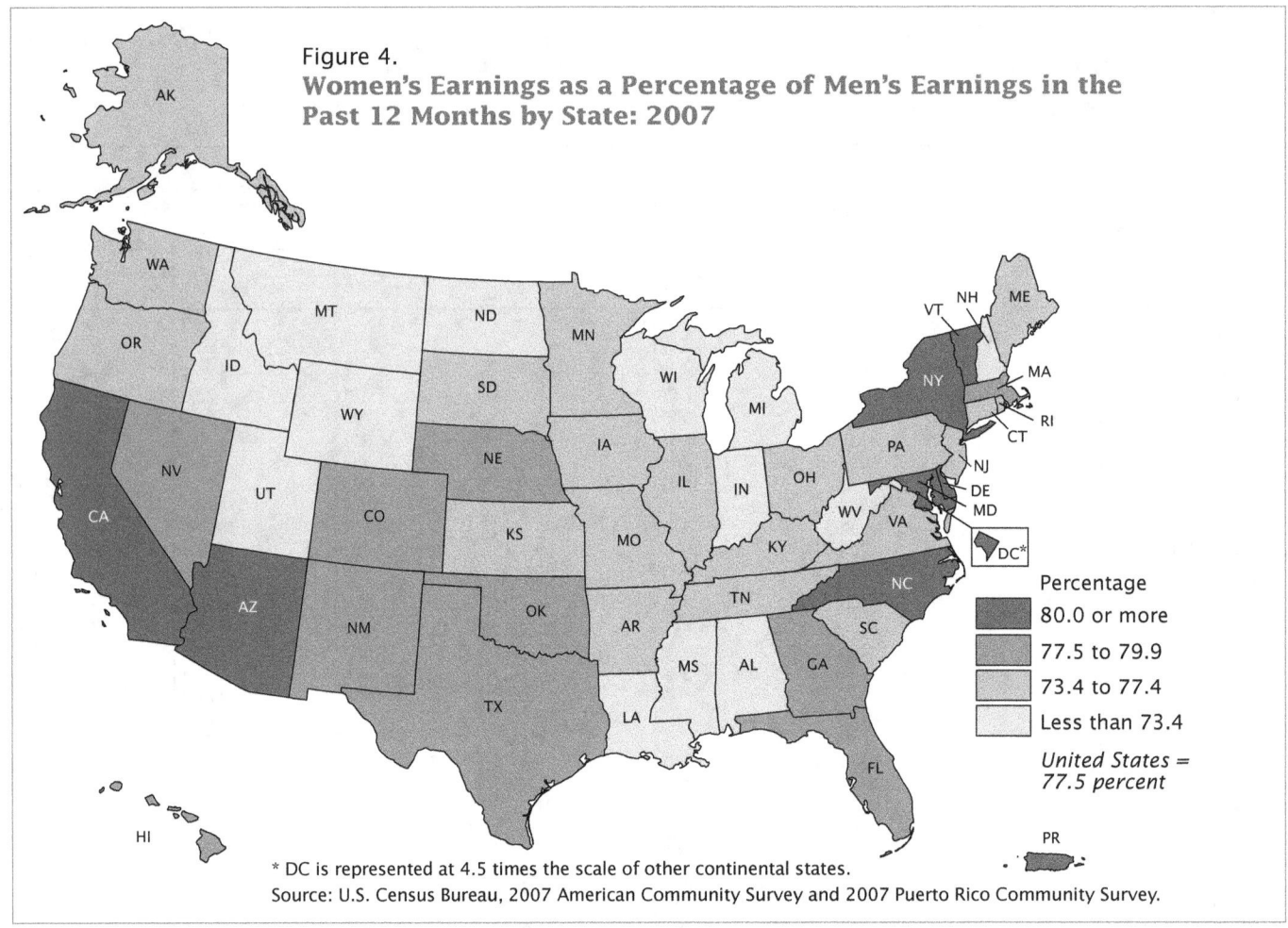

Figure 4.
Women's Earnings as a Percentage of Men's Earnings in the Past 12 Months by State: 2007

Percentage
80.0 or more
77.5 to 79.9
73.4 to 77.4
Less than 73.4

United States = 77.5 percent

* DC is represented at 4.5 times the scale of other continental states.
Source: U.S. Census Bureau, 2007 American Community Survey and 2007 Puerto Rico Community Survey.

Figure 4 displays the relationship between men's and women's earnings for all states and the District of Columbia. The Northeast, the South, and the West have states in which women's earnings as a percentage of men's earnings are relatively high (falling into the highest category in Figure 4). Every region has states in which the percentage was relatively low (falling into the two lower categories). In the South, five states (Maryland, North Carolina, Florida, Georgia, and Texas) and the District of Columbia had ratios higher than the national ratio, as did three states in the West (California, Arizona, and Colorado). Two states in the Northeast (Vermont and New York) had ratios higher than the national ratio. There were no

states in the Midwest that had ratios higher than the national ratio. As a result, women's earnings were closer to men's in more states in the South and the West than in the Northeast and the Midwest.

Median Earnings by Race and Hispanic Origin

Table 7 shows that Asian men working full-time, year-round had higher median earnings ($51,174) in the 2007 ACS than men in any of the other single-race groups. Non-Hispanic White men ($50,139) had higher earnings than Native Hawaiian and Other Pacific Islander men ($36,624), Black men ($35,652), and American Indian and

Alaska Native men ($34,833).[23] The lowest median earnings for men were for those who reported Some Other Race ($28,462). For Hispanic men, $29,239 was the median earnings.

The pattern observed for women by race was similar to that of men. Asian women had the highest median earnings ($40,664). Non-Hispanic White women ($36,398) had higher earnings than Black women ($31,035), Native Hawaiian and Other Pacific Islander women ($29,835), and American Indian and

---

[23] The median earnings of Native Hawaiian and Other Pacific Islander men were not statistically different from those of Black men and those of American Indian and Alaska Native men. The median earnings of Black men were not statistically different from those of American Indian and Alaska Native men.

Table 7.
Median Earnings in the Past 12 Months of Workers by Sex and Women's Earnings as a Percentage of Men's Earnings by Selected Characteristics for the United States: 2007

(In 2007 inflation-adjusted dollars. For information on confidentiality protection, sampling error, nonsampling error, and definitions, see www.census.gov/acs/www/)

| Selected characteristic | Median earnings (dollars) | | | | Women's earnings as a percentage of men's earnings | |
| | Men | | Women | | | |
	Estimate	Margin of error[1] (±)	Estimate	Margin of error[1] (±)	Estimate	Margin of error[1] (±)
Race and Hispanic Origin						
Full-time, year-round workers 16 years and older with earnings	44,255	147	34,278	85	77.5	0.3
White alone	47,113	93	35,542	64	75.4	0.2
White alone, not Hispanic	50,139	63	36,398	64	72.6	0.1
Black alone	35,652	179	31,035	127	87.1	0.5
American Indian and Alaska Native alone	34,833	932	28,837	693	82.8	2.7
Asian alone	51,174	292	40,664	317	79.5	0.7
Native Hawaiian and Other Pacific Islander alone	36,624	2,068	29,835	1,515	81.5	5.5
Some Other Race alone	28,462	350	24,801	234	87.1	1.1
Two or More Races	40,353	548	32,976	678	81.7	1.8
Hispanic (any race)	29,239	268	25,454	143	87.1	0.8
Educational Attainment						
Population 25 years and older with earnings	40,481	53	27,276	46	67.4	0.1
Less than high school graduate	22,602	137	14,202	116	62.8	0.7
High school graduate (includes equivalency)	32,435	63	21,219	54	65.4	0.2
Some college or associate's degree	41,035	83	27,046	69	65.9	0.2
Bachelor's degree	57,397	227	38,628	156	67.3	0.4
Graduate or professional degree	77,219	347	50,937	133	66.0	0.4
Industry						
Full-time, year-round civilian workers 16 years and older with earnings	44,627	151	34,393	85	77.1	0.3
Agriculture, forestry, fishing, and hunting	27,854	604	23,621	811	84.8	3.2
Mining	55,533	1,015	47,146	2,007	84.9	3.9
Construction	38,823	332	36,593	328	94.3	1.2
Manufacturing	45,954	191	32,535	262	70.8	0.6
Wholesale trade	45,767	367	36,187	402	79.1	1.0
Retail trade	35,721	211	25,959	131	72.7	0.6
Transportation and warehousing	46,052	240	37,145	381	80.7	1.0
Utilities	60,617	351	45,539	841	75.1	1.5
Information	58,964	1,282	43,614	691	74.0	2.1
Finance and insurance	71,422	406	39,390	297	55.2	0.6
Real estate and rental and leasing	43,314	1,024	36,959	396	85.3	2.2
Professional, scientific, and technical services	75,320	491	47,292	278	62.8	0.5
Management of companies and enterprises	76,630	3,691	47,715	1,598	62.3	3.6
Administrative and support and waste management services	31,706	223	28,973	444	91.4	1.6
Educational services	47,308	289	40,100	138	84.8	0.6
Health care and social assistance	50,258	299	33,477	179	66.6	0.5
Arts, entertainment, and recreation	35,953	447	30,293	331	84.3	1.3
Accommodation and food services	25,611	207	20,708	155	80.9	0.9
Other services (except public administration)	35,504	271	26,166	205	73.7	0.8
Public administration	54,545	348	41,936	222	76.9	0.6
Class of Worker[2]						
Full-time, year-round civilian workers 16 years and older with earnings	44,627	151	34,393	85	77.1	0.3
Employee of private company workers	42,215	81	32,035	60	75.9	0.2
Self-employed in own incorporated business workers	61,549	230	41,395	398	67.3	0.7
Private not-for-profit wage and salary workers	46,420	413	37,918	285	81.7	1.0
Local government workers	47,915	439	39,729	264	82.9	0.8
State government workers	48,778	440	38,584	303	79.1	0.8
Federal government workers	57,377	432	50,329	214	87.7	0.8
Self-employed in own unincorporated business workers	38,564	729	25,003	448	64.8	1.8

[1] Data are based on a sample and are subject to sampling variability. A margin of error is a measure of an estimate's variability. The larger the margin of error in relation to the size of the estimate, the less reliable the estimate. When added to and subtracted from the estimate, the margin of error forms the 90-percent confidence interval.
[2] Data from unpaid family workers are excluded from this table.

Source: U.S. Census Bureau, 2007 American Community Survey.

Alaska Native women ($28,837).[24] The lowest median earnings ($24,801) of any race group were for women of Some Other Race. Hispanic women had median earnings of $25,454.

For each of the race groups and Hispanics, as shown in Table 7, men had higher earnings than women. The group with the lowest female-to-male earnings ratio was non-Hispanic Whites, where women's earnings were 72.6 percent of men's earnings. The median earnings of women were at least 85 percent of men's for the Some Other Race group, Blacks, and Hispanics.[25]

Median Earnings by Educational Attainment

Data on median earnings by educational attainment in Table 7 are for all individuals 25 years and older with earnings and are not limited to full-time, year-round workers.

A person's level of education is a predictor of earnings—in general, the more education, the larger the earnings potential. Table 7 shows that this was true for both men and women in the 2007 ACS. The median earnings of men who were not high school graduates were $22,602. Median earnings were higher for male high school graduates ($32,435) and higher still for men with some college or an associate's degree ($41,035).

Men who completed college and received a bachelor's degree earned a median of $57,397. The highest median earnings among education groups, $77,219, were for men with a graduate or professional degree.

Women who did not complete high school reported median earnings of $14,202 in the 2007 ACS, while women who graduated from high school earned $21,219. Attending but not completing college, or receiving an associate's degree, resulted in median earnings of $27,046, while women who completed a bachelor's degree had median earnings of $38,628. As with men, women who received a graduate or professional degree earned the most, $50,937.

While both men and women showed higher earnings with higher levels of education, at each level of education, men earned more than women. The ratio of female-to-male earnings was lowest for those with less than a high school education, where women earned 62.8 percent of men. The ratio was higher among people with more education, up to the completion of a bachelor's degree. For men and women with a high school education, women earned 65.4 percent of what men earned, while women earned 65.9 percent when both had some college or an associate's degree. The ratio was higher still when both men and women had bachelor's degrees. At that educational level, women earned 67.3 percent of what men earned. Additional education beyond a bachelor's degree resulted in a lower earnings ratio. Women earned 66.0 percent

of men's earnings when both had a graduate or professional degree.[26]

Median Earnings by Industry and Class of Worker

Data on earnings by type of industry and class of worker are limited to full-time, year-round civilian workers 16 years or older. Industry refers to the kind of business conducted by a person's employing organization.

The industries for which data are collected in the ACS are commonly grouped into sectors. Table 7 shows the 20 major industry sectors. Men earned the most in the 2007 ACS in two of those sectors: the management of companies and enterprises sector ($76,630) and the professional, scientific, and technical services sector ($75,320).[27] Men in the accommodation and food services sector had the lowest median earnings ($25,611).

For women, several sectors had relatively high median earnings in the 2007 ACS. In the following sectors, women's median earnings were $45,000 or higher: management of companies and enterprises ($47,715); professional, scientific, and technical services ($47,292); mining ($47,146); and utilities

---

[24] The median earnings for Native Hawaiian and Other Pacific Islander women were not statistically different from those of Black women and those of American Indian and Alaska Native women.
[25] The female-to-male earnings ratio was not statistically different from 85 percent for Native Hawaiians and Other Pacific Islanders and American Indians and Alaska Natives.

[26] The female-to-male earnings ratio for workers with graduate or professional degrees was not statistically different from the ratio for workers with some college or associate's degrees.
[27] The median earnings for men in the management of companies and enterprises sector were not statistically different from the median earnings for men in the professional, scientific, and technical services sector.

($45,539).[28] As with men, the sector with the lowest earnings for women was accommodation and food services ($20,708).

In each of the 20 industry sectors, men earned more than women. The sector where the ratio between women's and men's earnings was the lowest was finance and insurance, where women's earnings were 55.2 percent of men's, while the highest ratio was in the construction sector, where women's earnings were 94.3 percent of men's.

Class of worker analysis categorizes employees according to the type of ownership of the organization employing them. Men who were employed in their own incorporated business and worked full-time, year-round had the highest median earnings at $61,549. Men employed in their own unincorporated business had the lowest median earnings ($38,564).

For women, those employed by the federal government had the highest median earnings at $50,329. Similar to men, those employed in their own unincorporated business had the lowest median earnings ($25,003).

For each of the class of worker categories shown in Table 7, men had higher earnings than women. The ratio of women's to men's earnings was highest for men and women

employed by the federal government (87.7). The ratio was lowest for women and men employed in their own businesses. When that business was unincorporated, women earned 64.8 percent of what men earned; when it was incorporated, they earned 67.3 percent of what men earned.

Median Earnings by Occupation

Occupation describes the kind of work that a person does on the job. Table 8 shows 26 occupation groups for full-time, year-round civilian workers. The large sample size of the ACS allows further examination of the earnings of men and women for many detailed occupations (see Appendix Table A-2).[29] Men earned the most in the legal occupations ($105,233) and the least in the food preparation and serving related occupations ($21,765). Women who worked in computer and mathematical occupations had the highest median earnings ($61,957). Women's median earnings in food preparation and serving related occupations ($18,060) were lower than all occupations except farming, fishing, and forestry occupations ($18,564).[30]

For women and men in the broad occupational groups shown in Table 8, men had higher median earnings than women. Installation, maintenance, and repair occupations and community and social services occupations had among the highest women's-to-men's earnings ratios, with a ratio of women's earnings to men's earnings higher than 90

percent. Within the community and social service occupations, the women's-to-men's earnings ratios ranged from 78.6 percent for religious workers to 94.2 percent for counselors.[31] In contrast, women's earnings as a percentage of men's earnings were 70 percent or less for legal occupations, health diagnosing, transportation supervisors and material moving workers, sales and related occupations, production occupations, motor vehicle operators, and personal care and service occupations. The legal occupation group had the lowest ratio of women's earnings to men's earnings (51.1 percent). There was less difference between women's and men's earnings among the detailed legal occupations. For example, Appendix Table A-2 shows that female paralegal and legal assistants earned 93.2 percent of what men earned and, for lawyers, the ratio was 77.8 percent.[32] Personal care and service workers, all other, was among the occupations with a high women's-to-men's earnings ratio, shown in Appendix Table A-2, at 111.3 percent, and the paper goods machine setters, operators, and tenders occupation was among the occupations with a low women's-to-men's earnings ratio, at 54.4 percent.[33]

[28] The median earnings of women in the management of companies and enterprises industry were not statistically different from the median earnings of women in the professional, scientific, and technical services industry and the mining industry, nor were the median earnings of women in the professional, scientific, and technical services industry statistically different from the median earnings of women in the mining industry. The median earnings of women in the utilities industry were not statistically different from the median earnings of women in the mining industry.

[29] Appendix Table A-2 is restricted to occupations with 100 or more sample cases and shows ratios for 283 out of 466 total occupations.

[30] The difference in women's median earnings between farming, fishing, and forestry occupations and building and grounds cleaning and maintenance occupations was not statistically significant.

[31] The women's-to-men's earnings ratio for religious workers was not statistically different from the ratio for community workers, clergy, or religious activities directors, nor was the ratio for counselors statistically different from that of social workers, clergy, and religious activities directors.

[32] The women's-to-men's earnings ratio for paralegal and legal assistants was not statistically different from the ratio for counselors. The women's-to-men's earnings ratio for lawyers was not statistically different from the ratio for religious workers.

[33] The personal care and service workers occupation was not statistically different from 41 other occupations with high earnings ratios. The paper goods machine setters, operators, and tenders occupation was not statistically different from 13 other low-earnings-ratio occupations.

Table 8.
Median Earnings in the Past 12 Months of Workers by Sex and Women's Earnings as a Percentage of Men's Earnings by Occupation for the United States: 2007

(In 2007 inflation-adjusted dollars. For information on confidentiality protection, sampling error, nonsampling error, and definitions, see *www.census.gov/acs/www/*)

Occupation	Median earnings (dollars)				Women's earnings as a percentage of men's earnings	
	Men		Women			
	Estimate	Margin of error[1] (±)	Estimate	Margin of error[1] (±)	Estimate	Margin of error[1] (±)
Full-time, year-round civilian workers 16 years and older with earnings	44,627	151	34,393	85	77.1	0.3
Management occupations	71,949	227	52,510	316	73.0	0.5
Business and financial operations occupations.	64,965	700	46,974	240	72.3	0.9
Computer and mathematical occupations.	71,980	297	61,957	402	86.1	0.7
Architecture and engineering occupations	70,606	296	56,627	830	80.2	1.2
Life, physical, and social science occupations	63,235	1,451	53,389	1,127	84.4	2.6
Community and social services occupations	40,677	325	37,173	264	91.4	1.0
Legal occupations	105,233	1,998	53,790	1,168	51.1	1.5
Education, training, and library occupations.	51,225	231	40,567	145	79.2	0.5
Arts, design, entertainment, sports, and media occupations	50,013	761	41,799	332	83.6	1.4
Health diagnosing and treating practitioners and other technical occupations.	100,451	507	59,318	483	59.1	0.6
Health technologists and technicians occupations	42,323	473	35,719	237	84.4	1.1
Healthcare support occupations	28,095	832	24,855	185	88.5	2.7
Fire fighting and prevention and other protective service workers, including supervisors occupations	40,266	422	31,997	528	79.5	1.6
Law enforcement workers, including supervisors occupations.	52,159	307	42,950	1,220	82.3	2.4
Food preparation and serving related occupations.	21,765	165	18,060	222	83.0	1.2
Building and grounds cleaning and maintenance occupations	26,291	191	19,093	200	72.6	0.9
Personal care and service occupations	30,575	369	21,256	154	69.5	1.0
Sales and related occupations	48,392	534	30,777	165	63.6	0.8
Office and administrative support occupations	36,466	175	31,173	65	85.5	0.4
Farming, fishing, and forestry occupations.	23,117	411	18,564	791	80.3	3.7
Construction and extraction occupations	35,771	169	32,011	657	89.5	1.9
Installation, maintenance, and repair occupations	41,472	128	40,325	982	97.2	2.4
Production occupations	36,565	137	24,722	191	67.6	0.6
Supervisors, transportation, and material moving workers, and other transportation workers except motor vehicle operators occupations	50,979	491	32,409	1,505	63.6	3.0
Motor vehicle operators occupations.	37,425	225	25,783	624	68.9	1.7
Material moving workers occupations	28,690	361	22,325	268	77.8	1.4

[1] Data are based on a sample and are subject to sampling variability. A margin of error is a measure of an estimate's variability. The larger the margin of error in relation to the size of the estimate, the less reliable the estimate. When added to and subtracted from the estimate, the margin of error forms the 90-percent confidence interval.

Source: U.S. Census Bureau, 2007 American Community Survey.

POVERTY

This section discusses poverty status for the nation, states, counties, and places and makes year-to-year comparisons in poverty-rate estimates between 2006 and 2007 for the states.[34] This section also discusses the depth of poverty for the nation and the states using the distribution of the population by income-to-poverty ratio. Official poverty, as defined by OMB's Statistical Policy Directive 14, uses a set of money income thresholds that vary by family size and composition but do not vary geographically—the Census Bureau uses the same threshold regardless of where a person or family resides.[35] The text box "How Is Poverty Calculated in the ACS?" provides a more detailed explanation of the poverty definition.

---

[34] The poverty universe is a subset of the total population covered by the ACS. Specifically, the universe excludes unrelated children under 15 years, people living in institutional group quarters, and those living in college dormitories or military barracks.

[35] The National Academy of Sciences Panel on Poverty and Family Assistance stated that the cost of housing varied across geographic areas, and the panel encouraged researchers to examine adjustments to poverty thresholds based on differences in housing costs. For examples of this work, see Charles Nelson and Kathleen Short, "The Distributional Implications of Geographic Adjustment of Poverty Thresholds" and Kathleen Short, "Where We Live—Geographic Differences in Poverty Thresholds," both available at <www.census.gov/hhes/www/povmeas/topicpg3.html>. In March 2008, Alemayehu Bishaw presented some preliminary estimates for adjusting the ACS poverty thresholds using a geographic index based on ACS gross rent data. The materials from the presentation at the Southern Regional Science Association Annual Meeting are available from the author on request.

How Is Poverty Calculated in the ACS?

Poverty statistics presented in this report and other ACS products adhere to the standards specified by the Office of Management and Budget in Statistical Policy Directive 14. The Census Bureau uses a set of dollar value thresholds that vary by family size and composition to determine who is in poverty. Further, poverty thresholds for people living alone or with nonrelatives (unrelated individuals) vary by age (under 65 years or 65 years and older). The poverty thresholds for two-person families also vary by the age of the householder. If a family's total income is less than the dollar value of the appropriate threshold, then that family and every individual in it are considered to be in poverty. Similarly, if an unrelated individual's total income is less than the appropriate threshold, then that individual is considered to be in poverty. The poverty thresholds do not vary geographically. They are updated annually to allow for changes in the cost of living (inflation factor) using the Consumer Price Index (CPI).

Since the ACS is a continuous survey, people respond throughout the year. Because the income items specify a period covering the last 12 months, the appropriate poverty thresholds are determined by multiplying the base-year poverty thresholds (1982) by the monthly inflation factor based on the 12 monthly CPIs and the base-year CPI.*

Example: Consider a family of three with one child under 18 years of age, interviewed in July 2007 and reporting a total family income of $14,000 for the previous 12 months (July 2006 to June 2007). The base-year (1982) threshold for such a family is $7,765, while the average of the 12 inflation factors is 2.11529. Multiplying $7,765 by 2.11529 determines the appropriate poverty threshold for this family, which is $16,425. Comparing the family's income of $14,000 with the poverty threshold shows that the family and all people in the family are considered to have been in poverty. The only difference for determining poverty status for unrelated individuals is that the person's individual total income is compared with the threshold. For further information on poverty data in the ACS, visit the Census Bureau's Web site at <www.census.gov/acs/www/usedata/Subject_Definitions.pdf>.

For information on poverty estimates from the ACS and how they differ from those based on the Current Population Survey Annual Social and Economic Supplement (CPS ASEC), which is the official source of poverty statistics for the United States, see "Guidance on Differences in Income and Poverty Estimates from Different Sources" at <www.census.gov/hhes/www/poverty/newguidance.html>. For a comparison of poverty rates and analysis of differences between the ACS and the CPS ASEC, see "A Comparison of the American Community Survey and the Current Population Survey" at <www.census.gov/hhes/www/poverty/acs_cpspovcompreport.pdf>.

* In 1982, the Census Bureau adopted a new poverty threshold matrix (as described above) that included the following changes from the original matrix: it eliminated the distinction between farm and nonfarm families and removed the separate thresholds for families with a female householder, no husband present.

Table 9.
Number and Percentage of People in Poverty in the Past 12 Months by Race and Hispanic Origin: 2007

(Numbers in thousands. For information on confidentiality protection, sampling error, nonsampling error, and definitions, see www.census.gov/acs/www/)

Race and Hispanic origin	All people for whom poverty status is determined[1]	2007			
		Below poverty			
		Number	Margin of error[2] (±)	Percentage	Margin of error[2] (±)
All races........................	293,744	38,052	233	13.0	0.1
White alone..................................	217,751	22,284	166	10.2	0.1
White alone, not Hispanic.................	193,759	17,404	142	9.0	0.1
Black alone..................................	35,681	8,807	77	24.7	0.2
American Indian and Alaska Native alone	2,278	576	19	25.3	0.8
Asian alone..................................	13,000	1,376	35	10.6	0.3
Native Hawaiian and Other Pacific Islander alone	422	66	7	15.7	1.5
Some Other Race alone	18,330	3,890	63	21.2	0.3
Two or More Races..........................	6,283	1,054	23	16.8	0.4
Hispanic (any race).........................	44,471	9,219	89	20.7	0.2

[1] Poverty status is determined for individuals in housing units and noninstitutional group quarters except people living in college dormitories or military barracks. Unrelated individuals under 15 years old are also excluded from the poverty universe.
[2] Data are based on a sample and are subject to sampling variability. A margin of error is a measure of an estimate's variability. The larger the margin of error in relation to the size of the estimate, the less reliable the estimate. When added to and subtracted from the estimate, the margin of error forms the 90-percent confidence interval.
Source: U.S. Census Bureau, 2007 American Community Survey.

Poverty Status for the United States by Race and Hispanic Origin

The 2007 ACS data show that an estimated 13.0 percent of the U.S. population had income below the poverty threshold in the past 12 months. Table 9 shows the number and percentage of people in poverty by race and Hispanic origin for 2007 with the margins of error.

At 9.0 percent, non-Hispanic Whites had the lowest percentage of people in poverty of all the groups presented in Table 9. The poverty rate for Asians was 10.6 percent. Native Hawaiians and Other Pacific Islanders had a poverty rate of 15.7 percent, which was lower than the rates for Blacks (24.7 percent) and American Indians and Alaska Natives (25.3 percent).[36]

The ACS includes reporting by people who chose Some Other Race or Two or More Races rather than one of the five single races named above. As presented in Table 9, the poverty rates for people who identified themselves as Some Other Race and Two or More Races were 21.2 percent and 16.8 percent, respectively.[37]

In the 2007 ACS, 20.7 percent of Hispanics (who may be any race) were in poverty.

Poverty Status for States

Table 10 shows the number and percentage of people in poverty in the past 12 months by state for the 2007 ACS. The map in Figure 5 displays the variation in poverty rates by state, while Appendix Figure B-1 shows a comparison of poverty rates by state with margins of error.

In the 2007 ACS, poverty rates among the 50 states and the District of Columbia varied from a low of 7.1 percent to a high of 20.6

percent (Table 10 and Appendix Figure B-1). Twenty-nine states had poverty rates lower than the estimated rate for the nation, while 17 states and the District of Columbia had rates higher than that of the nation.[38] At 7.1 percent, the poverty rate for New Hampshire was the lowest among all the states and the District of Columbia. At the other end of the distribution, Mississippi had the highest poverty rate, 20.6 percent, among all the states and the District of Columbia.

As shown in Table 10, twelve states (Alaska, California, Florida, Hawaii, Kansas, Missouri, New Hampshire, New York, Oklahoma, Pennsylvania, Texas, and Utah) and the District of Columbia had lower poverty rates in the 2007 ACS than in the 2006 ACS.[39] Ten of the states (Alaska, California, Florida, Hawaii,

---

[36] The poverty rates for Blacks and for American Indians and Alaska Natives were not statistically different from each other.

[37] The poverty rate for Native Hawaiians and Other Pacific Islanders was not statistically different from the poverty rate for people who identified themselves as Two or More Races.

[38] The poverty rates for Oregon, Missouri, South Dakota, and Ohio were not statistically different from the estimated poverty rate for the nation.

[39] All year-to-year comparisons using ACS data should be viewed with caution. See footnote 3 for more information.

Table 10.
Number and Percentage of People in Poverty in the Past 12 Months by State: 2006 and 2007

(Numbers in thousands. For information on confidentiality protection, sampling error, nonsampling error, and definitions, see *www.census.gov/acs/www/*)

Area	2006					2007					Change in poverty (2007 less 2006)	
	All people for whom poverty status is determined[1]	Below poverty				All people for whom poverty status is determined[1]	Below poverty					
		Number	Margin of error[2] (±)	Percentage	Margin of error[2] (±)		Number	Margin of error[2] (±)	Percentage	Margin of error[2] (±)	Number	Percentage
United States	291,531	38,757	222	13.3	0.1	293,744	38,052	223	13.0	0.1	*−705	*−0.3
Alabama	4,482	742	21	16.6	0.5	4,507	760	23	16.9	0.5	18	0.3
Alaska	652	71	7	10.9	1.1	667	60	5	8.9	0.8	*−11	*−2.0
Arizona	6,052	857	27	14.2	0.4	6,225	881	31	14.2	0.5	24	0.0
Arkansas	2,729	471	16	17.3	0.6	2,754	492	16	17.9	0.6	21	0.6
California	35,675	4,690	69	13.1	0.2	35,768	4,433	63	12.4	0.2	*−257	*−0.7
Colorado	4,653	556	18	12.0	0.4	4,756	569	20	12.0	0.4	13	0.0
Connecticut	3,393	280	13	8.3	0.4	3,388	269	13	7.9	0.4	−11	−0.4
Delaware	829	92	9	11.1	1.1	838	88	8	10.5	0.9	−4	−0.6
District of Columbia	551	108	8	19.6	1.4	560	92	8	16.4	1.4	*−16	*−3.2
Florida	17,686	2,227	42	12.6	0.2	17,847	2,159	39	12.1	0.2	*−68	*−0.5
Georgia	9,083	1,334	28	14.7	0.3	9,286	1,324	31	14.3	0.3	−10	−0.4
Hawaii	1,252	116	9	9.3	0.7	1,255	100	7	8.0	0.5	*−16	*−1.3
Idaho	1,432	180	8	12.6	0.6	1,464	178	9	12.1	0.6	−2	−0.5
Illinois	12,516	1,539	34	12.3	0.3	12,541	1,496	35	11.9	0.3	−43	−0.4
Indiana	6,126	778	24	12.7	0.4	6,145	758	20	12.3	0.3	−20	−0.4
Iowa	2,878	316	12	11.0	0.4	2,882	318	14	11.0	0.5	2	0.0
Kansas	2,680	331	12	12.4	0.5	2,689	300	13	11.2	0.5	*−31	*−1.2
Kentucky	4,087	693	20	17.0	0.5	4,121	714	22	17.3	0.5	21	0.3
Louisiana	4,165	793	24	19.0	0.6	4,167	775	20	18.6	0.5	−18	−0.4
Maine	1,286	166	9	12.9	0.7	1,281	154	8	12.0	0.6	−12	−0.9
Maryland	5,476	428	17	7.8	0.3	5,478	454	21	8.3	0.4	26	0.5
Massachusetts	6,236	620	19	9.9	0.3	6,245	621	21	9.9	0.3	1	0.0
Michigan	9,853	1,332	29	13.5	0.3	9,833	1,377	28	14.0	0.3	*45	*0.5
Minnesota	5,037	492	14	9.8	0.3	5,067	482	15	9.5	0.3	−10	−0.3
Mississippi	2,815	593	21	21.1	0.8	2,822	582	18	20.6	0.7	−11	−0.5
Missouri	5,674	770	23	13.6	0.4	5,709	742	20	13.0	0.4	−28	*−0.6
Montana	921	126	7	13.6	0.8	933	132	8	14.1	0.8	6	0.5
Nebraska	1,715	197	10	11.5	0.6	1,719	193	9	11.2	0.5	−4	−0.3
Nevada	2,461	254	13	10.3	0.5	2,529	270	17	10.7	0.7	16	0.4
New Hampshire	1,277	102	7	8.0	0.6	1,275	90	8	7.1	0.6	*−12	*−0.9
New Jersey	8,540	742	24	8.7	0.3	8,506	729	23	8.6	0.3	−13	−0.1
New Mexico	1,912	354	13	18.5	0.7	1,926	349	16	18.1	0.8	−5	−0.4
New York	18,770	2,662	41	14.2	0.2	18,775	2,570	42	13.7	0.2	*−92	*−0.5
North Carolina	8,591	1,261	29	14.7	0.3	8,793	1,259	29	14.3	0.3	−2	−0.4
North Dakota	606	69	5	11.4	0.8	613	74	5	12.1	0.9	5	0.7
Ohio	11,156	1,486	36	13.3	0.3	11,151	1,464	29	13.1	0.3	−22	−0.2
Oklahoma	3,462	588	18	17.0	0.5	3,498	557	17	15.9	0.5	*−31	*−1.1
Oregon	3,627	481	18	13.3	0.5	3,670	474	19	12.9	0.5	−7	−0.4
Pennsylvania	12,015	1,448	27	12.1	0.2	11,999	1,393	33	11.6	0.3	*−55	*−0.5
Rhode Island	1,026	114	9	11.1	0.8	1,019	122	9	12.0	0.9	8	0.9
South Carolina	4,183	656	20	15.7	0.5	4,270	642	20	15.0	0.5	−14	−0.7
South Dakota	753	102	7	13.6	0.9	768	101	6	13.1	0.8	−1	−0.5
Tennessee	5,878	952	27	16.2	0.4	5,997	954	29	15.9	0.5	2	−0.3
Texas	22,887	3,869	53	16.9	0.2	23,284	3,791	49	16.3	0.2	*−78	*−0.6
Utah	2,509	265	13	10.6	0.5	2,601	251	13	9.7	0.5	−14	*−0.9
Vermont	604	62	4	10.3	0.7	600	61	5	10.1	0.9	−1	−0.2
Virginia	7,404	709	22	9.6	0.3	7,466	743	23	9.9	0.3	*34	0.3
Washington	6,261	737	20	11.8	0.3	6,338	725	20	11.4	0.3	−12	−0.4
West Virginia	1,771	307	14	17.3	0.8	1,763	298	11	16.9	0.6	−9	−0.4
Wisconsin	5,401	592	19	11.0	0.3	5,447	588	18	10.8	0.3	−4	−0.2
Wyoming	500	47	5	9.4	1.0	509	44	6	8.7	1.2	−3	−0.7
Puerto Rico	3,865	1,753	31	45.4	0.8	3,878	1,763	27	45.5	0.7	10	0.1

* Statistically different from zero at the 90-percent confidence level.

[1] Poverty status is determined for individuals in housing units and noninstitutional group quarters except people living in college dormitories or military barracks. Unrelated individuals under 15 years old are also excluded from the poverty universe.

[2] Data are based on a sample and are subject to sampling variability. A margin of error is a measure of an estimate's variability. The larger the margin of error in relation to the size of the estimate, the less reliable the estimate. When added to and subtracted from the estimate, the margin of error forms the 90-percent confidence interval.

Source: U.S. Census Bureau, 2006 and 2007 American Community Surveys, and 2006 and 2007 Puerto Rico Community Surveys.

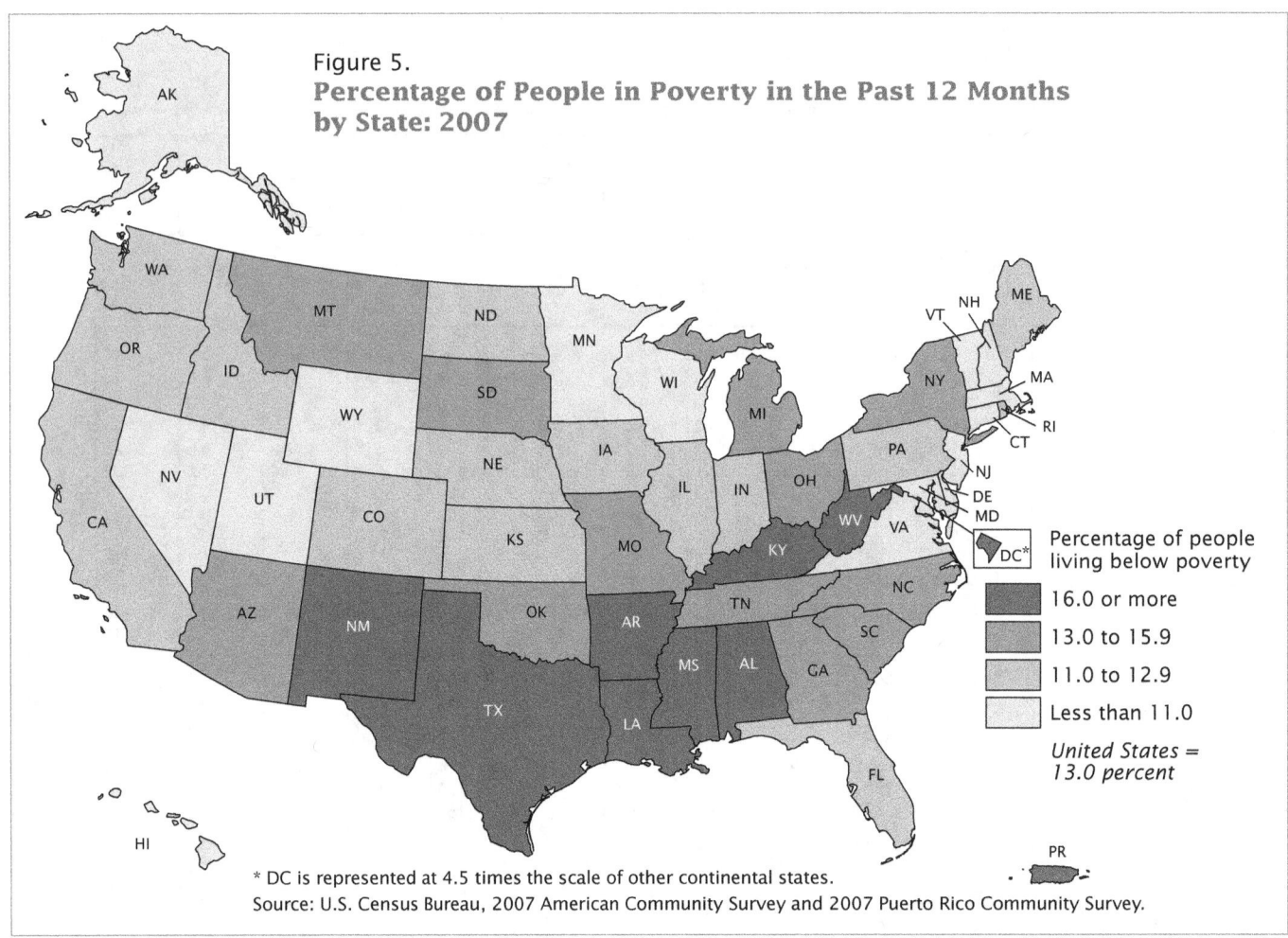

Figure 5.
Percentage of People in Poverty in the Past 12 Months by State: 2007

Percentage of people living below poverty

- 16.0 or more
- 13.0 to 15.9
- 11.0 to 12.9
- Less than 11.0

United States = 13.0 percent

* DC is represented at 4.5 times the scale of other continental states.
Source: U.S. Census Bureau, 2007 American Community Survey and 2007 Puerto Rico Community Survey.

Kansas, New Hampshire, New York, Oklahoma, Pennsylvania, and Texas) and the District of Columbia also had decreases in the number of people in poverty.

Michigan was the only state that had a higher poverty rate in the 2007 ACS than in the 2006 ACS, while Michigan and Virginia were the only states with an increase in the estimated number of people in poverty. At the same time, the changes in poverty rates for the rest of the states (37 states) were statistically undetectable.

For people living inside a metropolitan statistical area, the percentage of people in poverty was 12.4 percent in the 2007 ACS (Appendix Table B-1). For people in principal cities within metropolitan statistical areas, the poverty rate was 17.2

percent, while the rate for those not in principal cities within metropolitan statistical areas was 9.4 percent. Among the states, poverty rates for people living in principal cities within metropolitan statistical areas ranged from 6.5 percent to 23.7 percent, while the poverty rate for people within metropolitan statistical areas and not in principal cities ranged from 5.1 percent to 17.1 percent.[40] The ratio of the poverty rate for people not in principal cities within a metropolitan area to those in principal cities ranged from about 0.3 to about 1.1. Two states, Alaska and New Mexico, had ratios not

statistically different from 1— meaning the poverty rate for people living inside the principal cities was not statistically different from the poverty rate for people not living in principal cities within metropolitan statistical areas.[41]

Depth of Poverty

The poverty rate provides a measure of the proportion of people with family or individual income that is below the established poverty thresholds. The income-to-poverty ratio provides a measure to gauge the depth of poverty and to calculate the size of the population who might be eligible for government-sponsored assistance

[40] Two states (New Jersey and Rhode Island) and the District of Columbia have all of their population living in metropolitan statistical areas. Among the states, the lowest poverty rate for people living in principal cities within metropolitan statistical areas (6.5 percent) was not statistically different from the lowest poverty rate for people within metropolitan statistical areas and not in principal cities (5.1 percent).

[41] The ratio of the poverty rate for people not in principal cities within metropolitan statistical areas to those in principal cities for Alaska was not statistically different from those of three other states (New Mexico, Idaho, and Hawaii).

Figure 6.
Percentage of People by Income-to-Poverty Ratio in the Past 12 Months by State: 2007

(For information on confidentiality protection, sampling error, nonsampling error, and definitions, see *www.census.gov/acs/www/*)

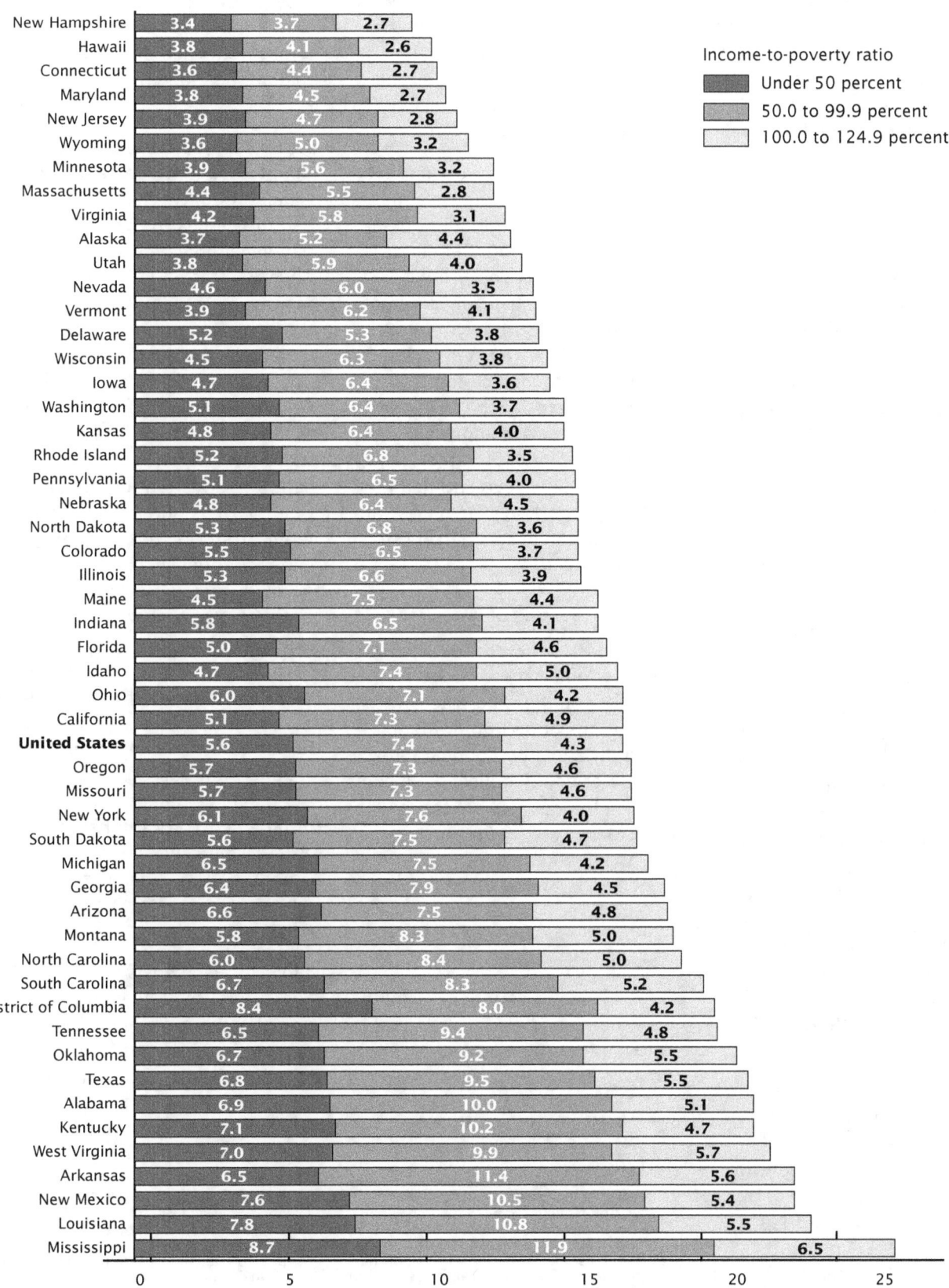

Income-to-poverty ratio
- Under 50 percent
- 50.0 to 99.9 percent
- 100.0 to 124.9 percent

State	Under 50	50.0 to 99.9	100.0 to 124.9
New Hampshire	3.4	3.7	2.7
Hawaii	3.8	4.1	2.6
Connecticut	3.6	4.4	2.7
Maryland	3.8	4.5	2.7
New Jersey	3.9	4.7	2.8
Wyoming	3.6	5.0	3.2
Minnesota	3.9	5.6	3.2
Massachusetts	4.4	5.5	2.8
Virginia	4.2	5.8	3.1
Alaska	3.7	5.2	4.4
Utah	3.8	5.9	4.0
Nevada	4.6	6.0	3.5
Vermont	3.9	6.2	4.1
Delaware	5.2	5.3	3.8
Wisconsin	4.5	6.3	3.8
Iowa	4.7	6.4	3.6
Washington	5.1	6.4	3.7
Kansas	4.8	6.4	4.0
Rhode Island	5.2	6.8	3.5
Pennsylvania	5.1	6.5	4.0
Nebraska	4.8	6.4	4.5
North Dakota	5.3	6.8	3.6
Colorado	5.5	6.5	3.7
Illinois	5.3	6.6	3.9
Maine	4.5	7.5	4.4
Indiana	5.8	6.5	4.1
Florida	5.0	7.1	4.6
Idaho	4.7	7.4	5.0
Ohio	6.0	7.1	4.2
California	5.1	7.3	4.9
United States	5.6	7.4	4.3
Oregon	5.7	7.3	4.6
Missouri	5.7	7.3	4.6
New York	6.1	7.6	4.0
South Dakota	5.6	7.5	4.7
Michigan	6.5	7.5	4.2
Georgia	6.4	7.9	4.5
Arizona	6.6	7.5	4.8
Montana	5.8	8.3	5.0
North Carolina	6.0	8.4	5.0
South Carolina	6.7	8.3	5.2
District of Columbia	8.4	8.0	4.2
Tennessee	6.5	9.4	4.8
Oklahoma	6.7	9.2	5.5
Texas	6.8	9.5	5.5
Alabama	6.9	10.0	5.1
Kentucky	7.1	10.2	4.7
West Virginia	7.0	9.9	5.7
Arkansas	6.5	11.4	5.6
New Mexico	7.6	10.5	5.4
Louisiana	7.8	10.8	5.5
Mississippi	8.7	11.9	6.5

Note: Details may not sum to totals because of rounding.

Source: U.S. Census Bureau, 2007 American Community Survey.

Income, Earnings, and Poverty Data From the 2007 American Community Survey

U.S. Census Bureau

programs, such as Temporary Assistance for Needy Families (TANF), Medicaid, food stamps, and the Low-Income Home Energy Assistance Program (LIHEAP). The income-to-poverty ratio is reported as a percentage, which compares a family's or individual's income relative to their poverty threshold. For example, a family or an individual with an income-to-poverty ratio of 110 percent has income that is 10 percent above their poverty threshold.

Appendix Table B-2 provides state-level estimates for the proportions of people with an income-to-poverty ratio that is less than 50 percent, less than 100 percent, and less than 125 percent. Figure 6 displays the percentage of the population with an income-to-poverty ratio less than 50 percent, 50 percent to less than 100 percent, and 100 percent to less than 125 percent. For purposes of comparison, both include estimates for the nation.

The 2007 ACS data show that 17.3 percent of the U.S. population had income below 125 percent of their poverty threshold. In Figure 6, people with income below 125 percent of their threshold are further divided into three groups based on their income-to-poverty ratios. Nationally, about 5.6 percent of people had income below 50 percent of their poverty threshold, 7.4 percent of people had income at or above 50 percent and less than 100 percent of their threshold, and 4.3 percent were at or above 100 percent of their threshold but below 125 percent of their threshold.

While not statistically different from each other, the following states were among the states with the lowest proportion of people with incomes less than 50 percent of their thresholds in the 2007 ACS: New Hampshire (3.4 percent), Connecticut (3.6 percent), Wyoming

(3.6 percent), Alaska (3.7 percent), Utah (3.8 percent), Hawaii (3.8 percent), and Vermont (3.9 percent). At the other end of the distribution, the proportion of people with income-to-poverty ratios less than 50 percent was 8.7 percent in Mississippi, higher than the other 49 states but not statistically different from the District of Columbia.[42]

About 17.3 percent of the population of the United States had an income-to-poverty ratio less than 125 percent, placing them in or near poverty (Appendix Table B-2). Although not statistically different from Hawaii, New Hampshire (9.8 percent) had a lower proportion of people with income-to-poverty ratios less than 125 percent than the other 48 states and the District of Columbia.[43] On the other hand, Mississippi (27.1 percent) had the highest proportion of people with income less than 125 percent of their threshold.

Poverty Status for Counties and Places

This section discusses poverty rates for counties and places with populations of 65,000 or more. Using the same two population-size categories as the household income section, larger areas are those with populations of 250,000 or more, and smaller areas are those with populations of 65,000 to less than 250,000.[44]

Poverty in Larger Areas

Table 11 shows counties or county equivalents and places with populations of 250,000 or more. This table

contains a list of the counties and places with ten of the highest and lowest poverty rates, together with their margins of error. In this table, the poverty rates for counties and places may not be statistically different from each other or from areas that are not shown.

Among the counties with a population of 250,000 or more, Cameron County, TX, (34.7 percent) and Hidalgo County, TX, (34.3 percent) had the highest proportions of people with income below their poverty thresholds in the past 12 months.[45] Among these large counties, the proportion of people with income below the poverty threshold in the past 12 months was lower for Douglas County, CO, (1.8 percent) than for all but one other county in the same size category. At 2.6 percent, the poverty rate for Somerset County, NJ, is not statistically different from Douglas County, CO.[46] Other counties included in the list of relatively low poverty rates had poverty rates that were, in many cases, not statistically different from each other. For example, the poverty rate for Loudon County, VA, at 3.1 percent, was not statistically different from those of Morris County, NJ, and Hamilton County, IN, both at 3.9 percent; Waukesha County, WI, (4.0 percent); Rockingham County, NH, (4.1 percent); and St. Charles County, MO, (4.2 percent)—all of which were not statistically different from each other.

Table 11 also shows that New York and Missouri had at least one county on the highest list and one on the lowest list. Among the large counties in New York, Nassau County (4.4 percent) and Suffolk County (5.0 percent) had lower poverty rates than other counties in

[42] The percentage of people with income-to-poverty ratios under 50 percent for the District of Columbia was not statistically different from the proportions for New Mexico and Louisiana.
[43] The percentages of people with income-to-poverty ratios under 125 percent for Hawaii, Connecticut, Maryland, and Wyoming were not statistically different from each other.
[44] Population size is based on the 2007 population estimates released as part of the Census Bureau's Population Estimates Program.

[45] The poverty rates for Hidalgo County, TX, and Cameron County, TX, were not statistically different from each other.
[46] The poverty rate for Somerset County, NJ, was not statistically different from that of Loudoun County, VA.

Table 11.
Percentage in Poverty in the Past 12 Months for Ten of the Highest and Lowest Poverty-Rate Counties and Places With 250,000 or More People: 2007

(For information on confidentiality protection, sampling error, nonsampling error, and definitions, see *www.census.gov/acs/www/*)

Area	Ten of the highest rates		Area	Ten of the lowest rates	
	Estimate[1]	Margin of error[2] (±)		Estimate[1]	Margin of error[2] (±)
Counties[3]			Counties[3]		
Cameron County, TX	34.7	2.5	Nassau County, NY...........	4.4	0.5
Hidalgo County, TX............	34.3	2.6	Johnson County, KS	4.2	0.6
El Paso County, TX............	28.7	1.7	St. Charles County, MO	4.2	0.8
Bronx County, NY	27.1	1.1	Rockingham County, NH	4.1	0.9
Philadelphia County, PA........	23.8	1.3	Waukesha County, WI.........	4.0	0.7
Tulare County, CA.............	23.7	2.3	Hamilton County, IN	3.9	1.0
Caddo Parish, LA	23.5	2.6	Morris County, NJ	3.9	1.0
St. Louis city, MO	22.4	2.0	Loudoun County, VA	3.1	0.8
Kings County, NY	21.9	0.8	Somerset County, NJ	2.6	0.6
Mobile County, AL.............	21.1	1.9	Douglas County, CO	1.8	0.6
Places[3]			Places[3]		
Detroit city, MI	33.8	1.4	San Diego city, CA	12.1	0.9
Cleveland city, OH.............	29.5	2.1	Las Vegas city, NV	11.9	1.5
Buffalo city, NY	28.7	2.5	Colorado Springs city, CO	11.8	1.5
El Paso city, TX..............	27.4	1.8	San Francisco city, CA	10.5	0.8
Memphis city, TN.............	26.2	1.9	Mesa city, AZ	10.2	1.4
Miami city, FL................	25.5	2.2	San Jose city, CA	9.9	1.0
Milwaukee city, WI............	24.4	1.4	Honolulu CDP, HI.............	8.6	1.1
Newark city, NJ	23.9	2.6	Anchorage municipality, AK	7.3	1.4
Philadelphia city, PA	23.8	1.3	Virginia Beach city, VA	6.4	1.1
Cincinnati city, OH............	23.5	2.1	Plano city, TX	5.9	1.4

[1] Poverty status is determined for individuals in housing units and noninstitutional group quarters except people living in college dormitories or military barracks. Unrelated individuals under 15 years old are also excluded from the poverty universe.
[2] Data are based on a sample and are subject to sampling variability. A margin of error is a measure of an estimate's variability. The larger the margin of error in relation to the size of the estimate, the less reliable the estimate. When added to and subtracted from the estimate, the margin of error forms the 90-percent confidence interval.
[3] Population size is based on the 2007 population estimates released as part of the U.S. Census Bureau's Population Estimates Program.

Note: Because of sampling variability, some of the estimates in this table may not be statistically different from one another or from estimates for other geographic areas not listed in the table.

Source: U.S. Census Bureau, 2007 American Community Survey.

the state, while Bronx County (27.1) had the highest poverty rate among similar-sized counties in the state.[47] The poverty rate for large counties in Missouri ranged from a low of 4.2 percent in St. Charles County to a high of 22.4 percent for St. Louis city.

Table 11 also shows that Detroit city, MI, had a higher proportion of people in poverty, at 33.8 percent, in the past 12 months than other places with populations of 250,000 or more. While not statistically different from each other, the poverty

rates for Cleveland city, OH, (29.5 percent); Buffalo city, NY, (28.7 percent); and El Paso city, TX, (27.4 percent), were higher than most other large places.[48] Among all the large places, Plano city, TX, (5.9 percent); Virginia Beach city, VA, (6.4 percent); and Anchorage municipality, AK, (7.3 percent) had percentages of people in poverty lower than other places of the same size.[49] The poverty rates for large places in Texas ranged from a low of 5.9 percent in

Plano city to a high of 27.4 percent in El Paso city.

Poverty in Smaller Areas

Table 12 presents data for ten of the highest and ten of the lowest poverty rates among counties and places with a population of 65,000 to less than 250,000. As noted with Table 11, the poverty rates for counties and places may not be statistically different from each other or from areas that are not shown.

Of the counties with 65,000 to 249,999 people, Apache County, AZ, (33.8 percent); St. Landry Parish, LA, (32.8 percent); Webb County, TX, (31.1 percent); and Robeson County, NC, (28.7 percent) had

---

[47] The poverty rate for Nassau County, NY, was not statistically different from the poverty rate for Suffolk County, NY, and the poverty rates for Nassau and Suffolk Counties in New York were not statistically different from that of St. Charles County, MO.

[48] The poverty rate for Buffalo city, NY, was not statistically different from the rate for El Paso city, TX; Memphis, TN; and Miami city, FL.
[49] The poverty rate for Plano city, TX; Virginia Beach city, VA; and Anchorage municipality, AK, were not statistically different from each other. Also, the poverty rate for Anchorage municipality, AK, was not statistically different from Honolulu CDP, HI.

Table 12.
Percentage in Poverty in the Past 12 Months for Ten of the Highest and Lowest Poverty-Rate Counties and Places With 65,000 to 249,999 People: 2007

(For information on confidentiality protection, sampling error, nonsampling error, and definitions, see *www.census.gov/acs/www/*)

Area	Ten of the highest rates		Area	Ten of the lowest rates	
	Estimate[1]	Margin of error[2] (±)		Estimate[1]	Margin of error[2] (±)
Counties[3]			Counties[3]		
Apache County, AZ	33.8	4.0	Sussex County, NJ	4.6	1.2
St. Landry Parish, LA	32.8	4.8	Delaware County, OH	4.5	1.2
Webb County, TX	31.1	3.3	Carroll County, MD	4.5	1.2
Clarke County, GA	28.7	3.0	Rockwall County, TX	4.5	2.0
Robeson County, NC	28.7	3.9	Hancock County, IN	4.2	1.7
Monroe County, IN	27.3	2.9	Scott County, MN	4.2	1.1
Brazos County, TX	27.3	2.8	Hunterdon County, NJ	4.1	0.8
Forrest County, MS	26.2	5.3	Kendall County, IL	3.9	1.4
Putnam County, TN	26.0	5.8	Carver County, MN	3.5	1.8
Bulloch County, GA	25.8	4.8	Stafford County, VA	3.4	1.2
Places[3]			Places[3]		
Bloomington city, IN	41.6	4.3	Overland Park city, KS	3.1	1.1
Camden city, NJ	38.2	5.6	Troy city, MI	3.1	1.2
Brownsville city, TX	36.5	3.6	Lakewood city, CA	3.0	1.9
Gainesville city, FL	36.0	4.1	Weston city, FL	2.3	1.5
Kalamazoo city, MI	35.5	4.1	Pleasanton city, CA	2.1	1.2
Flint city, MI	35.5	3.9	Flower Mound town, TX	1.9	1.2
Reading city, PA	34.5	4.7	Folsom city, CA	1.8	1.2
Macon city, GA	33.0	4.2	Yorba Linda city, CA	1.8	0.9
Youngstown city, OH	32.6	4.9	Chino city, CA	1.7	1.7
Pontiac city, MI	32.4	5.8	Highlands Ranch CDP, CO	0.8	0.6

[1] Poverty status is determined for individuals in housing units and noninstitutional group quarters except people living in college dormitories or military barracks. Unrelated individuals under 15 years old are also excluded from the poverty universe.
[2] Data are based on a sample and are subject to sampling variability. A margin of error is a measure of an estimate's variability. The larger the margin of error in relation to the size of the estimate, the less reliable the estimate. When added to and subtracted from the estimate, the margin of error forms the 90-percent confidence interval.
[3] Population size is based on the 2007 population estimates released as part of the U.S. Census Bureau's Population Estimates Program.

Note: Because of sampling variability, some of the estimates in this table may not be statistically different from one another or from estimates for other geographic areas not listed in the table.

Source: U.S. Census Bureau, 2007 American Community Survey.

among the higher point estimates of the proportion of people in poverty in the past 12 months. These estimates were not statistically different from each other. Furthermore, the poverty rates for Webb County, TX, and Robeson County, NC, were not statistically different from the rates of any other counties of comparable size presented in Table 12.[50] With point estimates ranging from 3.4 percent to 4.6 percent, the poverty rates for ten of the low-poverty small counties shown in Table 12 were not statistically different from each other. Texas had counties on both lists, with Rockwall County

having the lowest poverty rate (4.5 percent) among smaller counties in Texas, and Webb County (31.1 percent) and Brazos County (27.3 percent) having higher poverty rates than all counties of similar size in Texas.[51]

Table 12 also presents data for places with a population of 65,000 to less than 250,000 people. While not statistically different from Camden city, NJ; Brownsville city, TX; and Gainesville city, FL, the poverty rate for Bloomington city, IN, (41.6 percent) was higher than other smaller places. Table 12

shows 10 smaller places with low poverty rates that range from 0.8 percent to 3.1 percent. The apparent differences among these rates were not statistically significant except the poverty rate for Highlands Ranch CDP, CO, which was statistically different from those of Lakewood city, CA; Troy city, MI; and Overland Park city, KS. The poverty rate for Michigan, which has at least one place on the list of the highest and the list of the lowest poverty rates for small places, ranged from 3.1 percent in Troy city to 35.5 percent in both Kalamazoo city and Flint city.[52]

[50] The poverty rate for Webb County, TX, was not statistically different from St. Landry Parish, LA; Clarke County, GA; Robeson County, NC; Monroe County, IN; Brazos County, TX; Forrest County, MS; Putnam County, TN; and Bulloch County, GA.

[51] The poverty rates for Webb County and Brazos County in Texas were not statistically different from each other, and the poverty rates for Brazos County and Potter County in Texas were not statistically different from each other.

[52] The poverty rate for Troy city, MI, is not statistically different from the rates for Livonia city, MI, and West Bloomfield Township CDP, MI. The poverty rate for Kalamazoo city, MI, and Flint city, MI, were not statistically different from Pontiac city, MI.

SOURCE OF THE ESTIMATES

The data in this report are from the 2006 and 2007 ACS and the 2006 and 2007 Puerto Rico Community Surveys. The population covered in this report (the population universe) includes the population living in both households and group quarters. As described briefly in the introduction, different units of analysis are used for income and poverty in the different sections of this report. The section on household income does not include the group quarters population. The section on earnings includes all people 16 years and older regardless of living quarters (including people in households and all types of group quarters). The poverty universe excludes unrelated individuals under 15 years of age, people living in institutional group quarters, and people living in college dormitories and military barracks. The 2007 ACS estimated that 8.2 million people, or 2.7 percent of the total population, in the 50 states and the District of Columbia lived in group quarters. Of this population, 4.2 million lived in places classified as institutions and 2.3 million lived in college dormitories. Among people in group quarters, 15.5 percent were part of the poverty universe.

ACCURACY OF THE ESTIMATES

Statistics from surveys are subject to sampling and nonsampling error. Data from the ACS are based on a sample and are estimates of the actual figures that would have been obtained by interviewing the entire population using the same methodology. All comparisons presented in this report have taken sampling error into account and are significant at the 90-percent confidence level unless noted otherwise. This means the 90-percent confidence interval for the difference between the estimates being compared does not include zero. In this report, the 90-percent margins of error for the estimates are included in the tables in the columns labeled "Margin of error" and in Appendix Figures A-1 and B-1.

Nonsampling error in surveys may be attributed to a variety of sources, such as how the survey is designed, how respondents interpret questions, how able and willing they are to provide correct answers, and how accurately the answers are keyed, coded, edited, and classified. Nonsampling errors in the ACS may affect the data in two ways. Errors that are introduced randomly increase the variability of the estimates. Systematic errors consistent in one direction introduce bias into the results. The Census Bureau protects against systematic errors by conducting extensive research and evaluation programs on sampling techniques, questionnaire design, and data collection and processing procedures.

The final ACS population estimates are adjusted in the weighting procedure for coverage error by controlling specific survey estimates to independent population controls by sex, age, race, and Hispanic origin. This weighting partially corrects for bias due to over- or undercoverage, but biases may still be present, for example, when people who were missed differ from those interviewed in ways other than sex, age, race, and Hispanic origin. How this weighting procedure affects other variables in the survey is not precisely known. All of these considerations affect comparisons across different surveys or data sources.

For information on sampling and estimation methods, confidentiality protection, and sampling and nonsampling errors, please see the "2007 ACS Accuracy of the Data" document located at <www.census.gov/acs/www/Downloads/ACS/accuracy2007.pdf>.

Measures of ACS quality—including sample size and number of interviews, response and nonresponse rates, coverage rates, and item allocation rates—are available at <www.census.gov/acs/www/UseData/sse/index.htm>.

Figure A-1.
Median Household Income in the Past 12 Months With Margins of Error by State: 2007

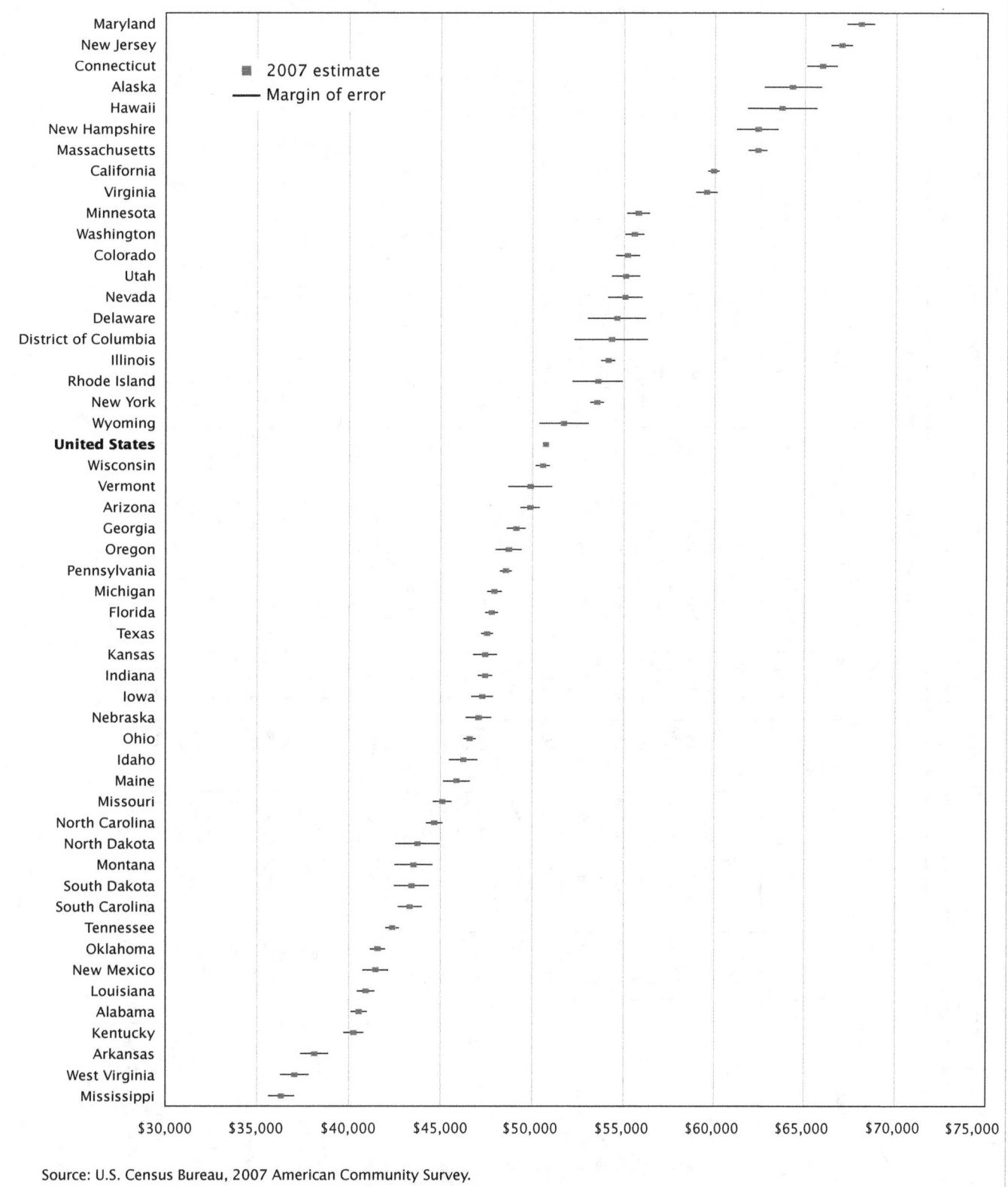

Source: U.S. Census Bureau, 2007 American Community Survey.

(In 2007 inflation-adjusted dollars. For information on confidentiality protection, sampling error, nonsampling error, and definitions, see *www.census.gov/acs/www/*)

Area	Total		In metropolitan or micropolitan statistical area												Not in metropolitan or micropolitan statistical area	
			In metropolitan statistical area						In micropolitan statistical area							
			Total		In principal city		Not in principal city		Total		In principal city		Not in principal city			
	Median	Margin of error[1] (±)	Median	Margin of error[1] (±)	Median	Margin of error[1] (±)	Median	Margin of error[1] (±)	Median	Margin of error[1] (±)	Median	Margin of error[1] (±)	Median	Margin of error[1] (±)	Median	Margin of error[1] (±)
United States	51,658	78	53,066	112	45,590	148	58,772	157	41,367	195	35,962	328	44,136	240	37,844	267
Alabama	41,507	490	42,491	598	37,644	993	45,891	984	37,182	1,312	34,521	1,903	38,291	1,685	31,315	1,287
Alaska	67,272	2,179	67,509	2,280	66,577	2,814	68,867	2,340	(B)	(B)	(B)	(B)	(B)	(B)	55,395	2,558
Arizona	50,263	437	50,697	448	46,951	798	55,415	892	40,082	2,300	41,349	3,695	39,041	2,715	36,061	3,001
Arkansas	40,443	613	42,309	777	40,018	1,462	44,932	1,201	35,046	1,016	32,952	1,676	36,357	1,338	30,400	948
California	60,090	215	60,363	203	56,977	362	62,682	411	43,450	1,610	36,436	3,056	45,951	2,158	44,563	2,818
Colorado	56,129	689	56,369	681	46,101	844	65,621	895	51,224	2,879	44,191	5,040	53,940	5,445	45,541	1,660
Connecticut	65,967	815	66,313	963	51,973	1,214	73,801	1,163	63,023	2,197	(B)	(B)	67,700	3,073	(X)	(X)
Delaware	54,610	1,581	55,841	2,372	38,203	2,865	60,547	2,342	50,976	2,532	(B)	(B)	51,276	2,455	(X)	(X)
District of Columbia	54,317	1,984	54,317	1,984	54,317	1,984	(X)	(X)	(X)	(X)	(X)	(X)	(X)	(X)	(X)	(X)
Florida	48,010	343	48,489	360	43,753	512	50,554	381	39,664	1,419	40,010	3,202	39,603	1,578	39,091	2,778
Georgia	50,667	370	52,143	395	40,695	827	55,770	491	36,744	1,189	29,811	2,123	40,448	1,524	35,038	1,219
Hawaii	63,757	1,924	65,367	1,776	55,536	2,737	75,621	2,450	60,879	2,156	60,096	3,801	61,123	2,588	(B)	(B)
Idaho	46,822	874	48,223	904	43,879	1,992	51,666	998	42,365	1,555	40,085	3,080	43,542	2,233	42,384	2,553
Illinois	55,035	361	56,710	385	47,615	757	62,837	607	41,035	813	33,273	1,843	45,961	1,055	41,240	1,155
Indiana	47,795	400	48,861	507	39,863	792	55,586	678	43,815	887	35,808	950	49,092	1,068	42,904	1,476
Iowa	49,090	801	50,724	586	43,373	1,056	60,234	1,085	43,964	1,643	40,039	1,374	49,945	1,977	43,464	881
Kansas	49,250	791	52,766	923	44,796	982	61,945	1,126	40,398	1,210	37,604	1,984	43,351	2,316	40,324	1,020
Kentucky	43,050	710	46,048	699	41,345	1,003	49,381	942	35,114	1,167	31,545	1,749	37,218	1,479	31,317	893
Louisiana	41,421	463	43,458	696	38,252	1,029	47,751	1,041	33,657	1,182	27,274	2,502	36,802	1,384	33,637	2,113
Maine	49,472	965	50,449	912	42,135	2,993	53,109	1,255	44,398	3,528	(B)	(B)	49,653	2,181	38,149	1,349
Maryland	68,512	748	68,852	791	46,438	1,274	74,455	908	62,332	4,265	(B)	(B)	67,701	2,444	48,546	4,202
Massachusetts	62,334	506	62,334	506	49,963	1,139	67,785	742	(X)	(X)	(X)	(X)	(X)	(X)	(B)	(B)
Michigan	49,325	425	50,148	367	39,041	765	55,506	495	43,077	1,099	34,246	1,874	45,966	1,045	38,055	755
Minnesota	58,252	716	60,931	668	51,921	895	65,179	866	46,561	1,132	40,716	1,732	51,162	948	43,374	812
Mississippi	38,380	894	43,940	1,083	33,727	2,517	48,217	1,554	31,875	1,077	26,420	1,607	35,539	1,506	30,315	902
Missouri	47,132	510	49,532	615	38,049	1,164	55,097	632	38,126	1,095	33,698	1,354	40,596	923	34,804	1,020
Montana	45,988	1,411	45,535	2,000	43,123	1,896	50,125	2,304	46,428	1,790	41,906	2,654	51,473	4,746	38,941	1,530
Nebraska	49,388	813	51,989	868	46,048	1,091	65,727	2,126	42,223	1,221	39,892	1,667	47,252	1,922	39,756	1,227
Nevada	55,052	929	55,412	932	51,917	928	58,907	1,284	50,280	2,714	48,776	3,280	52,439	3,763	(B)	(B)
New Hampshire	63,209	1,374	69,027	2,066	56,171	3,462	74,644	2,420	54,279	2,400	48,324	5,011	56,424	2,075	(B)	(B)

See footnotes at end of table.

Table A-1.
Median Household Income in the Past 12 Months by Metropolitan or Micropolitan Statistical Area Status and State: 2007—Con.

(In 2007 inflation-adjusted dollars. For information on confidentiality protection, sampling error, nonsampling error, and definitions, see www.census.gov/acs/www/)

Area	Total		In metropolitan or micropolitan statistical area											Not in metropolitan or micropolitan statistical area	
			In metropolitan statistical area						In micropolitan statistical area						
			Total		In principal city		Not in principal city		Total		In principal city		Not in principal city		
	Median	Margin of error[1] (±)	Median	Margin of error[1] (±)	Median	Margin of error[1] (±)	Median	Margin of error[1] (±)	Median	Margin of error[1] (±)	Median	Margin of error[1] (±)	Median	Margin of error[1] (±)	Median	Margin of error[1] (±)
New Jersey	67,035	573	67,035	573	45,437	1,847	69,892	759	(X)	(X)	(X)	(X)	(X)	(X)	(X)	(X)
New Mexico	41,907	700	43,985	1,160	42,758	1,515	45,792	1,766	37,400	1,371	37,140	1,778	37,817	2,163	27,429	3,678
New York	53,834	345	54,974	373	45,748	513	67,381	525	42,466	791	34,355	1,758	45,941	992	44,824	1,350
North Carolina	45,629	468	47,438	594	45,749	856	48,907	715	40,373	613	34,360	1,742	42,102	734	34,758	1,248
North Dakota	45,349	1,291	45,346	1,722	38,958	2,351	58,826	2,515	45,353	1,868	42,678	3,563	(B)	(B)	40,377	1,533
Ohio	46,887	324	47,740	462	35,043	606	54,237	569	42,497	835	35,372	1,450	46,318	884	40,791	864
Oklahoma	42,719	547	44,884	622	40,691	835	49,147	923	37,293	945	34,166	1,131	40,732	929	35,498	982
Oregon	49,235	701	51,277	556	46,193	958	55,709	964	40,931	1,129	37,907	2,229	42,715	1,563	39,056	1,901
Pennsylvania	49,026	317	50,378	241	33,784	693	56,054	375	41,555	682	30,643	1,693	43,575	786	38,357	870
Rhode Island	53,568	1,353	53,568	1,353	46,662	2,999	57,896	2,311	(X)	(X)	(X)	(X)	(X)	(X)	(X)	(X)
South Carolina	44,570	669	45,778	637	39,329	1,423	47,274	762	39,197	1,670	38,895	3,475	39,285	1,909	29,556	2,028
South Dakota	45,258	1,183	47,488	1,407	45,636	2,015	50,119	2,123	40,787	1,866	35,956	3,588	48,868	2,358	38,664	1,969
Tennessee	43,732	457	45,779	433	40,111	734	51,140	700	36,444	827	32,014	1,832	38,240	1,182	33,170	1,588
Texas	48,376	324	49,319	325	42,924	426	57,477	589	37,675	859	34,095	1,478	42,309	1,564	36,664	732
Utah	55,911	749	56,569	774	41,917	1,272	62,327	932	46,565	2,171	42,100	3,374	51,394	3,093	40,878	2,027
Vermont	51,414	1,169	56,879	2,858	(B)	(B)	61,570	2,715	47,918	1,712	(B)	(B)	50,771	2,365	45,122	2,004
Virginia	62,323	431	63,559	662	51,747	807	70,462	699	42,466	1,908	39,449	2,693	43,592	2,851	38,634	1,363
Washington	56,356	506	57,903	714	50,292	851	62,998	815	44,314	1,872	36,085	2,240	48,633	1,635	39,487	1,835
West Virginia	39,033	1,006	40,480	883	34,678	2,469	41,877	914	35,237	1,822	32,931	4,621	35,757	2,153	31,723	1,107
Wisconsin	51,908	404	52,427	496	41,325	770	60,988	585	49,239	1,196	39,958	1,823	52,954	1,245	42,913	906
Wyoming	55,317	2,573	49,598	2,670	47,496	2,889	(B)	(B)	58,890	3,247	54,811	4,788	64,958	5,507	46,715	2,718
Puerto Rico	17,833	383	17,990	399	20,174	761	17,395	400	13,895	1,700	(B)	(B)	15,017	2,262	(B)	(B)

(B) Data for territories below the population of 65,000 are not published as single-year estimates by the American Community Survey.
(X) Not applicable. Indicates states that do not contain any territory in micropolitan statistical areas and/or do not contain any territory outside of metropolitan or micropolitan statistical areas.
[1] Data are based on a sample and are subject to sampling variability. A margin of error is a measure of an estimate's variability. The larger the margin of error in relation to the size of the estimate, the less reliable the estimate. When added to and subtracted from the estimate, the margin of error forms the 90-percent confidence interval.

Source: U.S. Census Bureau, 2007 American Community Survey and 2007 Puerto Rico Community Survey.

Table A-2.
Median Earnings in the Past 12 Months of Workers by Sex and Women's Earnings as a Percentage of Men's Earnings by Detailed Occupation for the United States: 2007

(In 2007 inflation-adjusted dollars. For information on confidentiality protection, sampling error, nonsampling error, and definitions, see www.census.gov/acs/www/)

Occupation	Median earnings (dollars)				Women's earnings as a percentage of men's earnings[1]	
	Men		Women			
	Estimate	Margin of error[2] (±)	Estimate	Margin of error[2] (±)	Estimate	Margin of error[2] (±)
Management Occupations						
Chief executives	116,800	3,000	90,300	4,381	77.3	4.2
General and operations managers	75,200	1,594	55,500	1,589	73.8	2.6
Legislators	66,300	8,574	(B)	(B)	(X)	(X)
Advertising and promotions managers	70,800	4,879	50,300	4,300	71.1	7.8
Marketing and sales managers	90,300	1,186	60,200	2,020	66.7	2.4
Public relations managers	81,100	2,765	61,600	3,639	76.0	5.2
Administrative services managers	63,100	1,949	52,300	2,862	82.8	5.2
Computer and information systems managers	91,200	826	80,800	1,504	88.6	1.8
Financial managers	86,000	1,393	51,300	428	59.7	1.1
Human resources managers	71,500	962	60,600	765	84.8	1.6
Industrial production managers	70,500	1,653	57,100	5,167	81.1	7.6
Purchasing managers	73,900	3,423	56,000	1,230	75.8	3.9
Transportation, storage, and distribution managers	46,300	1,342	44,600	5,540	96.3	12.3
Farm, ranch, and other agricultural managers	40,500	406	31,900	3,075	78.7	7.6
Farmers and ranchers	30,400	145	17,600	2,064	57.9	6.8
Construction managers	61,800	1,449	53,000	1,444	85.7	3.1
Education administrators	73,800	1,821	54,200	1,740	73.4	3.0
Engineering managers	106,900	2,597	96,700	8,421	90.5	8.2
Food service managers	40,500	270	30,400	192	75.0	0.7
Funeral directors	55,700	3,670	35,700	2,385	64.2	6.0
Gaming managers	48,700	5,053	(B)	(B)	(X)	(X)
Lodging managers	44,500	4,175	35,600	1,688	80.0	8.4
Medical and health services managers	76,500	1,640	60,500	630	79.0	1.9
Natural sciences managers	108,700	21,622	(B)	(B)	(X)	(X)
Postmasters and mail superintendents	65,800	2,586	53,500	2,025	81.3	4.4
Property, real estate, and community association managers	55,700	2,907	40,100	1,522	72.0	4.6
Social and community service managers	60,600	1,936	46,900	1,711	77.5	3.8
Managers, all other	76,000	308	56,200	474	74.0	0.7
Business and Financial Operations Occupations						
Agents and business managers of artists, performers, and athletes	51,400	3,851	43,700	6,113	84.9	13.5
Purchasing agents and buyers, farm products	50,900	3,270	(B)	(B)	(X)	(X)
Wholesale and retail buyers, except farm products	45,400	972	39,100	1,653	86.0	4.1
Purchasing agents, except wholesale, retail, and farm products	52,200	2,058	44,700	1,772	85.7	4.8
Claims adjusters, appraisers, examiners, and investigators	51,400	1,555	41,300	1,379	80.3	3.6
Compliance officers, except agriculture, construction, health and safety, and transportation	60,600	1,306	50,900	975	84.0	2.4
Cost estimators	58,900	2,945	45,000	5,305	76.4	9.8
Human resources, training, and labor relations specialists	57,700	2,492	46,200	479	80.1	3.6
Logisticians	57,300	4,076	46,300	4,395	80.8	9.6
Management analysts	82,100	1,290	64,900	2,236	79.0	3.0
Meeting and convention planners	(B)	(B)	46,100	614	(X)	(X)
Other business operations specialists	53,900	3,700	40,600	426	75.4	5.2
Accountants and auditors	69,900	1,892	47,600	824	68.0	2.2
Appraisers and assessors of real estate	55,200	4,043	40,100	3,260	72.7	8.0
Budget analysts	68,800	6,017	60,800	1,660	88.4	8.1

See footnotes at end of table.

Income, Earnings, and Poverty Data From the 2007 American Community Survey

U.S. Census Bureau

Table A-2.
Median Earnings in the Past 12 Months of Workers by Sex and Women's Earnings as a Percentage of Men's Earnings by Detailed Occupation for the United States: 2007—Con.

(In 2007 inflation-adjusted dollars. For information on confidentiality protection, sampling error, nonsampling error, and definitions, see www.census.gov/acs/www/)

Occupation	Median earnings (dollars)				Women's earnings as a percentage of men's earnings[1]	
	Men		Women			
	Estimate	Margin of error[2] (±)	Estimate	Margin of error[2] (±)	Estimate	Margin of error[2] (±)
Business and Financial Operations Occupations—Con.						
Credit analysts	49,900	4,550	40,800	1,477	81.8	8.0
Financial analysts	92,200	11,454	60,800	2,806	65.9	8.7
Personal financial advisors	88,600	5,438	51,900	2,027	58.5	4.3
Insurance underwriters	66,200	5,453	45,400	1,760	68.6	6.2
Financial examiners	76,700	10,285	(B)	(B)	(X)	(X)
Loan counselors and officers	61,500	711	42,700	944	69.4	1.7
Tax examiners, collectors, and revenue agents	50,700	3,547	41,500	2,255	81.9	7.3
Tax preparers	63,200	12,624	40,500	3,176	64.1	13.8
Financial specialists, all other	71,000	4,667	41,100	3,566	58.0	6.3
Computer and Mathematical Occupations						
Computer scientists and systems analysts	70,800	778	61,400	620	86.7	1.3
Computer programmers	72,000	773	67,500	2,245	93.8	3.3
Computer software engineers	86,900	689	75,700	1,135	87.1	1.5
Computer support specialists	50,700	566	47,600	2,221	93.8	4.5
Database administrators	76,900	2,691	59,400	3,619	77.3	5.4
Network and computer systems administrators	63,500	1,735	56,500	2,453	89.0	4.6
Network systems and data communications analysts	63,400	2,454	55,200	2,652	87.0	5.4
Actuaries	101,800	12,546	(B)	(B)	(X)	(X)
Operations research analysts	77,700	3,576	60,800	804	78.3	3.7
Statisticians	81,800	5,980	65,400	3,879	80.0	7.5
Architecture and Engineering Occupations						
Architects, except naval	71,400	977	55,400	3,359	77.5	4.8
Surveyors, cartographers, and photogrammetrists	53,200	4,458	(B)	(B)	(X)	(X)
Aerospace engineers	87,300	1,425	76,300	4,195	87.5	5.0
Biomedical engineers	73,100	6,736	(B)	(B)	(X)	(X)
Chemical engineers	87,600	4,586	75,700	7,546	86.5	9.7
Civil engineers	76,700	712	64,000	2,287	83.4	3.1
Computer hardware engineers	84,500	4,853	70,200	16,332	83.1	19.9
Electrical and electronic engineers	82,100	1,533	72,000	2,963	87.7	4.0
Environmental engineers	72,900	5,308	(B)	(B)	(X)	(X)
Industrial engineers, including health and safety	71,300	620	59,000	4,178	82.9	5.9
Marine engineers and naval architects	77,700	8,569	(B)	(B)	(X)	(X)
Materials engineers	70,200	2,727	(B)	(B)	(X)	(X)
Mechanical engineers	71,900	671	68,800	4,057	95.7	5.7
Petroleum engineers	102,800	7,317	(B)	(B)	(X)	(X)
Engineers, all other	81,800	610	71,900	3,747	87.9	4.6
Drafters	45,800	452	38,700	1,416	84.4	3.2
Engineering technicians, except drafters	51,100	257	40,500	859	79.2	1.7
Surveying and mapping technicians	41,100	648	(B)	(B)	(X)	(X)
Life, Physical, and Social Science Occupations						
Agricultural and food scientists	61,500	4,042	(B)	(B)	(X)	(X)
Biological scientists	55,100	2,647	51,000	2,158	92.6	5.9
Conservation scientists and foresters	55,200	2,757	(B)	(B)	(X)	(X)
Medical scientists	70,700	3,501	64,200	4,011	90.8	7.2
Astronomers and physicists	95,300	6,741	(B)	(B)	(X)	(X)
Atmospheric and space scientists	70,800	12,662	(B)	(B)	(X)	(X)
Chemists and materials scientists	66,500	3,203	59,200	3,751	89.1	7.1

See footnotes at end of table.

Median Earnings in the Past 12 Months of Workers by Sex and Women's Earnings as a Percentage of Men's Earnings by Detailed Occupation for the United States: 2007—Con.

(In 2007 inflation-adjusted dollars. For information on confidentiality protection, sampling error, nonsampling error, and definitions, see *www.census.gov/acs/www/*)

Occupation	Median earnings (dollars)				Women's earnings as a percentage of men's earnings[1]	
	Men		Women			
	Estimate	Margin of error[2] (±)	Estimate	Margin of error[2] (±)	Estimate	Margin of error[2] (±)
Life, Physical, and Social Science Occupations—Con.						
Environmental scientists and geoscientists	73,100	4,159	52,400	3,438	71.6	6.2
Physical scientists, all other	81,800	2,221	62,800	2,525	76.8	3.7
Economists	102,800	6,082	(B)	(B)	(X)	(X)
Market and survey researchers	77,500	4,530	58,700	3,736	75.7	6.5
Psychologists	71,000	1,759	57,800	2,788	81.4	4.4
Urban and regional planners	61,600	4,341	56,100	4,710	91.1	10.0
Miscellaneous social scientists and related workers	56,000	9,324	45,800	7,509	81.8	19.1
Agricultural and food science technicians	39,900	5,104	32,400	5,529	81.3	17.3
Biological technicians	47,600	4,963	39,900	7,355	84.0	17.8
Chemical technicians	51,800	2,020	42,800	2,351	82.5	5.6
Geological and petroleum technicians	50,900	9,039	(B)	(B)	(X)	(X)
Other life, physical, and social science technicians	41,600	2,186	37,500	2,316	90.1	7.3
Community and Social Services Occupations						
Counselors	40,500	388	38,100	813	94.2	2.2
Social workers	41,100	753	38,300	485	93.1	2.1
Miscellaneous community and social service specialists	41,500	1,387	34,800	999	84.0	3.7
Clergy	39,400	1,045	35,100	1,629	89.1	4.8
Directors, religious activities and education	40,400	2,099	35,900	2,101	88.8	7.0
Religious workers, all other	39,200	3,960	30,800	2,782	78.6	10.7
Legal Occupations						
Lawyers	120,400	2,071	93,600	3,897	77.8	3.5
Judges, magistrates, and other judicial workers	108,100	6,825	69,500	4,159	64.3	5.6
Paralegals and legal assistants	45,700	1,469	42,600	475	93.2	3.2
Miscellaneous legal support workers	56,000	3,989	40,700	544	72.7	5.3
Education, Training, and Library Occupations						
Postsecondary teachers	66,000	911	51,900	1,101	78.6	2.0
Preschool and kindergarten teachers	(B)	(B)	22,900	847	(X)	(X)
Elementary and middle school teachers	47,300	531	43,000	168	91.0	1.1
Secondary school teachers	49,600	957	44,700	1,082	90.1	2.8
Special education teachers	45,300	2,425	42,900	1,306	94.7	5.8
Other teachers and instructors	46,600	2,395	35,200	1,087	75.6	4.5
Archivists, curators, and museum technicians	48,100	4,344	42,800	3,566	89.0	10.9
Librarians	50,400	1,701	45,800	561	91.0	3.3
Library technicians	(B)	(B)	29,600	1,793	(X)	(X)
Teacher assistants	27,600	2,528	18,400	186	66.8	6.1
Other education, training, and library workers	51,200	1,601	47,700	3,721	93.1	7.8
Arts, Design, Entertainment, Sports, and Media Occupations						
Artists and related workers	47,600	3,512	39,800	3,106	83.5	9.0
Designers	50,500	638	39,100	1,296	77.5	2.7
Producers and directors	56,500	6,258	52,500	3,772	92.9	12.3
Athletes, coaches, umpires, and related workers	42,300	3,267	35,100	2,642	83.0	9.0
Musicians, singers, and related workers	39,000	3,716	35,200	1,063	90.1	9.0
Announcers	40,300	3,711	(B)	(B)	(X)	(X)
News analysts, reporters, and correspondents	51,300	2,191	42,300	3,163	82.4	7.1
Public relations specialists	65,900	5,772	50,700	821	76.9	6.9
Editors	52,900	2,527	46,300	1,995	87.5	5.6
Technical writers	63,700	4,233	57,300	4,121	89.9	8.8

See footnotes at end of table.

Median Earnings in the Past 12 Months of Workers by Sex and Women's Earnings as a Percentage of Men's Earnings by Detailed Occupation for the United States: 2007—Con.

(In 2007 inflation-adjusted dollars. For information on confidentiality protection, sampling error, nonsampling error, and definitions, see www.census.gov/acs/www/)

Occupation	Median earnings (dollars)				Women's earnings as a percentage of men's earnings[1]	
	Men		Women			
	Estimate	Margin of error[2] (±)	Estimate	Margin of error[2] (±)	Estimate	Margin of error[2] (±)
Arts, Design, Entertainment, Sports, and Media Occupations—Con.						
Writers and authors	53,500	3,803	48,300	3,213	90.4	8.8
Miscellaneous media and communication workers	40,700	2,568	35,600	1,943	87.5	7.3
Broadcast and sound engineering technicians and radio operators	47,200	2,683	(B)	(B)	(X)	(X)
Photographers	41,000	2,013	28,800	1,856	70.3	5.7
Television, video, and motion picture camera operators and editors	45,500	2,494	(B)	(B)	(X)	(X)
Healthcare Practitioner and Technical Occupations						
Chiropractors	81,800	6,939	45,700	12,336	55.9	15.8
Dentists	150,500	9,334	102,500	9,678	68.1	7.7
Dietitians and nutritionists	(B)	(B)	41,300	2,548	(X)	(X)
Optometrists	102,700	5,351	(B)	(B)	(X)	(X)
Pharmacists	103,000	1,657	100,300	1,397	97.4	2.1
Physicians and surgeons	181,200	2,959	115,000	7,203	63.5	4.1
Physician assistants	77,000	6,463	49,300	6,070	64.0	9.5
Registered nurses	63,100	2,617	57,900	668	91.7	3.9
Audiologists	(B)	(B)	60,200	8,781	(X)	(X)
Occupational therapists	63,900	5,068	56,900	2,132	89.1	7.8
Physical therapists	69,400	2,104	61,200	571	88.2	2.8
Radiation therapists	(B)	(B)	68,200	3,688	(X)	(X)
Respiratory therapists	55,400	1,826	47,700	2,405	86.2	5.2
Speech-language pathologists	(B)	(B)	55,700	893	(X)	(X)
Therapists, all other	48,600	4,374	41,100	1,387	84.5	8.1
Veterinarians	96,100	7,909	71,100	2,425	74.0	6.6
Clinical laboratory technologists and technicians	45,700	1,489	40,700	214	89.1	2.9
Dental hygienists	(B)	(B)	50,800	595	(X)	(X)
Diagnostic related technologists and technicians	55,400	3,152	49,100	735	88.7	5.2
Emergency medical technicians and paramedics	41,800	1,987	32,600	1,719	78.0	5.5
Health diagnosing and treating practitioner support technicians	34,700	1,724	28,200	757	81.3	4.6
Licensed practical and licensed vocational nurses	35,900	1,387	35,700	286	99.6	3.9
Medical records and health information technicians	(B)	(B)	25,600	441	(X)	(X)
Opticians, dispensing	39,100	3,196	31,400	2,846	80.3	9.8
Miscellaneous health technologists and technicians	42,900	3,976	32,700	1,477	76.2	7.8
Other healthcare practitioners and technical occupations	51,400	3,038	43,200	4,780	84.0	10.5
Healthcare Support Occupations						
Nursing, psychiatric, and home health aides	26,500	724	23,300	169	88.1	2.5
Physical therapist assistants and aides	37,700	6,363	35,600	1,275	94.4	16.3
Massage therapists	(B)	(B)	28,400	3,144	(X)	(X)
Dental assistants	(B)	(B)	28,800	1,331	(X)	(X)
Medical assistants and other healthcare support occupations	30,300	355	25,900	665	85.5	2.4

See footnotes at end of table.

Median Earnings in the Past 12 Months of Workers by Sex and Women's Earnings as a Percentage of Men's Earnings by Detailed Occupation for the United States: 2007—Con.

(In 2007 inflation-adjusted dollars. For information on confidentiality protection, sampling error, nonsampling error, and definitions, see www.census.gov/acs/www/)

Occupation	Median earnings (dollars)				Women's earnings as a percentage of men's earnings[1]	
	Men		Women			
	Estimate	Margin of error[2] (±)	Estimate	Margin of error[2] (±)	Estimate	Margin of error[2] (±)
Protective Service Occupations						
First-line supervisors/managers of correctional officers	48,500	3,277	45,500	5,835	93.9	13.6
First-line supervisors/managers of police and detectives ...	70,800	1,175	51,000	4,316	72.0	6.2
First-line supervisors/managers of fire fighting and prevention workers	73,100	4,361	(B)	(B)	(X)	(X)
Supervisors, protective service workers, all other	44,200	3,007	40,800	697	92.3	6.5
Fire fighters	57,100	2,099	51,300	2,444	89.9	5.4
Fire inspectors	51,000	4,330	(B)	(B)	(X)	(X)
Bailiffs, correctional officers, and jailers	41,000	411	35,300	740	86.2	2.0
Detectives and criminal investigators	68,900	3,696	51,300	2,731	74.5	5.6
Police and sheriff's patrol officers	54,400	1,328	50,600	1,839	93.0	4.1
Animal control workers	(B)	(B)	28,800	2,739	(X)	(X)
Private detectives and investigators	54,600	4,030	40,900	2,257	74.9	6.9
Security guards and gaming surveillance officers	30,100	540	28,300	1,122	93.9	4.1
Lifeguards and other protective service workers	34,300	4,336	25,000	2,005	72.8	10.9
Food Preparation and Serving Related Occupations						
Chefs and head cooks	30,600	326	25,200	924	82.5	3.1
First-line supervisors/managers of food preparation and serving workers	27,600	1,568	21,400	892	77.4	5.5
Cooks	20,200	94	16,500	513	81.3	2.6
Food preparation workers	18,400	518	16,800	951	91.5	5.8
Bartenders	25,600	844	20,500	719	80.1	3.9
Combined food preparation and serving workers, including fast food	20,300	528	16,300	538	80.2	3.4
Counter attendants, cafeteria, food concession, and coffee shop	18,400	2,716	15,400	885	83.7	13.3
Waiters and waitresses	22,100	892	17,900	704	81.0	4.6
Food servers, nonrestaurant	23,600	2,374	19,400	1,096	82.4	9.5
Dining room and cafeteria attendants and bartender helpers	17,900	957	16,400	1,020	91.8	7.5
Dishwashers	16,300	222	15,200	571	93.1	3.7
Hosts and hostesses, restaurant, lounge, and coffee shop	(B)	(B)	18,100	933	(X)	(X)
Building and Grounds Cleaning and Maintenance Occupations						
First-line supervisors/managers of housekeeping and janitorial workers	38,700	1,117	25,300	398	65.5	2.2
First-line supervisors/managers of landscaping, lawn service, and groundskeeping workers	36,600	1,691	29,100	3,598	79.6	10.5
Janitors and building cleaners	26,400	178	20,100	155	76.1	0.8
Maids and housekeeping cleaners	22,200	701	17,400	265	78.6	2.8
Pest control workers	32,900	1,811	(B)	(B)	(X)	(X)
Grounds maintenance workers	21,900	890	20,400	844	93.1	5.4

See footnotes at end of table.

Table A-2.
Median Earnings in the Past 12 Months of Workers by Sex and Women's Earnings as a Percentage of Men's Earnings by Detailed Occupation for the United States: 2007—Con.

(In 2007 inflation-adjusted dollars. For information on confidentiality protection, sampling error, nonsampling error, and definitions, see *www.census.gov/acs/www/*)

Occupation	Median earnings (dollars)				Women's earnings as a percentage of men's earnings[1]	
	Men		Women			
	Estimate	Margin of error[2] (±)	Estimate	Margin of error[2] (±)	Estimate	Margin of error[2] (±)
Personal Care and Service Occupations						
First-line supervisors/managers of gaming workers	40,800	869	33,800	2,584	82.9	6.6
First-line supervisors/managers of personal service workers	40,500	535	26,300	893	65.0	2.4
Animal trainers	29,300	6,175	28,000	4,371	95.5	25.1
Nonfarm animal caretakers	28,300	3,652	21,900	3,302	77.6	15.4
Gaming services workers	37,500	2,956	33,400	2,875	89.0	10.4
Miscellaneous entertainment attendants and related workers	24,700	1,545	21,000	2,173	85.3	10.3
Barbers	25,200	1,030	20,900	1,783	82.9	7.9
Hairdressers, hairstylists, and cosmetologists	32,800	3,227	22,500	676	68.7	7.1
Miscellaneous personal appearance workers	21,300	3,604	20,400	253	95.8	16.3
Baggage porters, bellhops, and concierges	28,300	2,722	26,400	3,958	93.3	16.6
Tour and travel guides	28,200	4,395	(B)	(B)	(X)	(X)
Transportation attendants	41,000	1,163	33,900	2,706	82.7	7.0
Child care workers	23,100	2,709	17,300	257	74.8	8.9
Personal and home care aides	23,100	1,469	19,600	564	85.1	5.9
Recreation and fitness workers	35,700	1,043	26,700	1,633	74.9	5.1
Residential advisors	25,400	2,663	24,500	2,242	96.6	13.4
Personal care and service workers, all other	23,500	3,446	26,200	2,162	111.3	18.7
Sales and Related Occupations						
First-line supervisors/managers of retail sales workers	42,300	658	30,400	120	71.9	1.2
First-line supervisors/managers of non-retail sales workers	56,400	658	46,300	1,267	82.1	2.4
Cashiers	23,600	1,110	18,100	173	76.9	3.7
Counter and rental clerks	33,600	3,356	20,500	1,918	61.0	8.4
Parts salespersons	33,700	1,109	25,200	1,392	74.6	4.8
Retail salespersons	35,900	239	23,600	648	65.9	1.9
Advertising sales agents	60,400	2,783	45,700	1,614	75.7	4.4
Insurance sales agents	63,600	4,787	37,600	1,513	59.1	5.0
Securities, commodities, and financial services sales agents	85,900	5,285	49,400	3,104	57.5	5.1
Travel agents	36,300	2,331	32,200	1,194	88.6	6.6
Sales representatives, services, all other	61,300	503	50,300	1,336	82.1	2.3
Sales representatives, wholesale and manufacturing	61,100	339	50,500	627	82.6	1.1
Models, demonstrators, and product promoters	(B)	(B)	26,400	1,630	(X)	(X)
Real estate brokers and sales agents	60,400	2,102	43,200	2,724	71.6	5.2
Sales engineers	85,800	5,226	(B)	(B)	(X)	(X)
Telemarketers	25,400	4,057	21,500	1,762	84.6	15.2
Door-to-door sales workers, news and street vendors, and related workers	30,500	1,226	24,600	2,686	80.9	9.4
Sales and related workers, all other	60,400	2,134	42,800	1,972	70.9	4.1
Office and Administrative Support Occupations						
First-line supervisors/managers of office and administrative support workers	48,900	748	38,600	380	78.9	1.4
Switchboard operators, including answering service	(B)	(B)	25,400	1,165	(X)	(X)
Telephone operators	(B)	(B)	26,700	2,352	(X)	(X)
Bill and account collectors	32,700	972	30,400	229	92.9	2.8
Billing and posting clerks and machine operators	35,900	1,923	29,800	505	83.1	4.7
Bookkeeping, accounting, and auditing clerks	38,400	1,426	32,100	360	83.7	3.2
Payroll and timekeeping clerks	37,700	3,175	34,400	931	91.1	8.0

See footnotes at end of table.

Median Earnings in the Past 12 Months of Workers by Sex and Women's Earnings as a Percentage of Men's Earnings by Detailed Occupation for the United States: 2007—Con.

(In 2007 inflation-adjusted dollars. For information on confidentiality protection, sampling error, nonsampling error, and definitions, see www.census.gov/acs/www/)

Occupation	Median earnings (dollars)				Women's earnings as a percentage of men's earnings[1]	
	Men		Women			
	Estimate	Margin of error[2] (±)	Estimate	Margin of error[2] (±)	Estimate	Margin of error[2] (±)
Office and Administrative Support Occupations—Con.						
Procurement clerks	55,300	3,469	37,500	1,926	67.8	5.5
Tellers	24,300	985	22,600	235	92.9	3.9
Court, municipal, and license clerks	41,600	1,601	31,400	1,365	75.6	4.4
Credit authorizers, checkers, and clerks	43,700	8,562	32,300	1,755	74.0	15.1
Customer service representatives	34,900	957	30,100	252	86.2	2.5
Eligibility interviewers, government programs	42,100	4,649	37,000	1,515	87.8	10.3
File clerks	31,400	2,291	28,500	507	90.9	6.8
Hotel, motel, and resort desk clerks	22,900	1,453	20,400	342	89.1	5.8
Interviewers, except eligibility and loan	32,600	5,517	27,400	1,326	84.2	14.8
Library assistants, clerical	(B)	(B)	25,300	582	(X)	(X)
Loan interviewers and clerks	40,700	1,367	35,300	956	86.6	3.7
New accounts clerks	(B)	(B)	29,600	2,877	(X)	(X)
Order clerks	30,700	436	28,200	943	91.9	3.3
Human resources assistants, except payroll and timekeeping	(B)	(B)	33,700	2,319	(X)	(X)
Receptionists and information clerks	30,300	786	25,300	156	83.5	2.2
Reservation and transportation ticket agents and travel clerks	39,000	3,310	32,600	1,694	83.6	8.3
Information and record clerks, all other	36,400	5,415	30,700	438	84.4	12.6
Cargo and freight agents	40,400	888	(B)	(B)	(X)	(X)
Couriers and messengers	38,900	1,974	30,300	2,088	78.0	6.7
Dispatchers	38,900	1,505	30,900	676	79.4	3.5
Meter readers, utilities	36,500	3,775	(B)	(B)	(X)	(X)
Postal service clerks	50,200	477	48,000	1,068	95.5	2.3
Postal service mail carriers	51,000	265	47,100	951	92.4	1.9
Postal service mail sorters, processors, and processing machine operators	50,700	387	48,300	525	95.4	1.3
Production, planning, and expediting clerks	50,900	620	35,700	883	70.2	1.9
Shipping, receiving, and traffic clerks	29,500	666	25,200	260	85.5	2.1
Stock clerks and order fillers	25,500	160	23,400	360	91.6	1.5
Weighers, measurers, checkers, and samplers, recordkeeping	35,900	2,342	25,600	1,622	71.1	6.5
Secretaries and administrative assistants	36,200	1,344	32,000	293	88.5	3.4
Computer operators	42,500	2,341	33,800	1,841	79.6	6.2
Data entry keyers	30,800	1,109	28,700	426	93.3	3.6
Word processors and typists	32,700	2,441	30,400	196	92.9	7.0
Insurance claims and policy processing clerks	35,800	1,171	30,900	760	86.2	3.5
Mail clerks and mail machine operators, except postal service	28,600	1,408	25,500	513	89.3	4.8
Office clerks, general	34,600	1,778	30,100	268	87.0	4.5
Office machine operators, except computer	30,700	1,308	25,800	1,115	84.1	5.1
Statistical assistants	(B)	(B)	35,100	1,531	(X)	(X)
Office and administrative support workers, all other	41,300	1,546	34,500	748	83.7	3.6
Farming, Fishing, and Forestry Occupations						
First-line supervisors/managers of farming, fishing, and forestry workers	36,700	2,671	(B)	(B)	(X)	(X)
Agricultural inspectors	45,900	2,627	(B)	(B)	(X)	(X)
Graders and sorters, agricultural products	26,600	6,863	18,400	2,091	69.3	19.6
Miscellaneous agricultural workers	20,900	722	17,300	360	82.5	3.3
Fishers and related fishing workers	30,200	4,113	(B)	(B)	(X)	(X)
Forest and conservation workers	35,600	8,886	(B)	(B)	(X)	(X)
Logging workers	30,000	1,675	(B)	(B)	(X)	(X)

See footnotes at end of table.

Table A-2.
Median Earnings in the Past 12 Months of Workers by Sex and Women's Earnings as a Percentage of Men's Earnings by Detailed Occupation for the United States: 2007—Con.

(In 2007 inflation-adjusted dollars. For information on confidentiality protection, sampling error, nonsampling error, and definitions, see *www.census.gov/acs/www/*)

Occupation	Median earnings (dollars)				Women's earnings as a percentage of men's earnings[1]	
	Men		Women			
	Estimate	Margin of error[2] (±)	Estimate	Margin of error[2] (±)	Estimate	Margin of error[2] (±)
Construction and Extraction Occupations						
First-line supervisors/managers of construction trades and extraction workers	50,800	234	43,000	5,307	84.8	10.5
Boilermakers	49,400	3,849	(B)	(B)	(X)	(X)
Brickmasons, blockmasons, and stonemasons	30,500	541	(B)	(B)	(X)	(X)
Carpenters	31,900	670	27,400	4,122	86.0	13.1
Carpet, floor, and tile installers and finishers	30,500	308	(B)	(B)	(X)	(X)
Cement masons, concrete finishers, and terrazzo workers	30,200	1,666	(B)	(B)	(X)	(X)
Construction laborers	27,700	847	25,100	1,415	90.5	5.8
Paving, surfacing, and tamping equipment operators	31,800	6,239	(B)	(B)	(X)	(X)
Operating engineers and other construction equipment operators	39,000	1,351	(B)	(B)	(X)	(X)
Drywall installers, ceiling tile installers, and tapers	26,500	750	(B)	(B)	(X)	(X)
Electricians	42,200	883	33,900	4,912	80.4	11.8
Glaziers	35,500	972	(B)	(B)	(X)	(X)
Insulation workers	32,300	3,070	(B)	(B)	(X)	(X)
Painters, construction and maintenance	27,200	1,255	25,200	873	92.9	5.4
Pipelayers, plumbers, pipefitters, and steamfitters	40,400	299	(B)	(B)	(X)	(X)
Plasterers and stucco masons	26,500	1,750	(B)	(B)	(X)	(X)
Roofers	26,500	1,895	(B)	(B)	(X)	(X)
Sheet metal workers	36,900	1,301	(B)	(B)	(X)	(X)
Structural iron and steel workers	42,400	3,093	(B)	(B)	(X)	(X)
Helpers, construction trades	21,300	1,209	(B)	(B)	(X)	(X)
Construction and building inspectors	48,700	1,344	45,300	4,687	93.1	10.0
Elevator installers and repairers	66,500	6,799	(B)	(B)	(X)	(X)
Fence erectors	26,300	3,377	(B)	(B)	(X)	(X)
Hazardous materials removal workers	36,400	2,907	(B)	(B)	(X)	(X)
Highway maintenance workers	34,500	1,120	(B)	(B)	(X)	(X)
Rail-track laying and maintenance equipment operators	48,700	5,358	(B)	(B)	(X)	(X)
Septic tank servicers and sewer pipe cleaners	35,400	2,449	(B)	(B)	(X)	(X)
Miscellaneous construction and related workers	33,400	3,601	(B)	(B)	(X)	(X)
Derrick, rotary drill, and service unit operators, oil, gas, and mining	53,500	5,756	(B)	(B)	(X)	(X)
Earth drillers, except oil and gas	40,600	1,798	(B)	(B)	(X)	(X)
Explosives workers, ordnance handling experts, and blasters	40,700	7,220	(B)	(B)	(X)	(X)
Mining machine operators	50,800	480	(B)	(B)	(X)	(X)
Other extraction workers	45,600	3,170	(B)	(B)	(X)	(X)
Installation, Maintenance, and Repair Occupations						
First-line supervisors/managers of mechanics, installers, and repairers	51,700	1,671	48,100	3,821	93.0	8.0
Computer, automated teller, and office machine repairers	42,500	1,048	40,100	2,112	94.4	5.5
Radio and telecommunications equipment installers and repairers	52,200	1,852	52,700	3,042	101.0	6.8
Avionics technicians	48,600	5,859	(B)	(B)	(X)	(X)
Electric motor, power tool, and related repairers	45,800	1,406	(B)	(B)	(X)	(X)
Electrical and electronics repairers, industrial and utility	60,800	1,313	(B)	(B)	(X)	(X)

See footnotes at end of table.

Table A-2.
Median Earnings in the Past 12 Months of Workers by Sex and Women's Earnings as a Percentage of Men's Earnings by Detailed Occupation for the United States: 2007—Con.

(In 2007 inflation-adjusted dollars. For information on confidentiality protection, sampling error, nonsampling error, and definitions, see www.census.gov/acs/www/)

Occupation	Median earnings (dollars)				Women's earnings as a percentage of men's earnings[1]	
	Men		Women			
	Estimate	Margin of error[2] (±)	Estimate	Margin of error[2] (±)	Estimate	Margin of error[2] (±)
Installation, Maintenance, and Repair Occupations—Con.						
Electronic equipment installers and repairers, motor vehicles	45,600	6,682	(B)	(B)	(X)	(X)
Electronic home entertainment equipment installers and repairers	36,500	2,800	(B)	(B)	(X)	(X)
Security and fire alarm systems installers	40,800	790	(B)	(B)	(X)	(X)
Aircraft mechanics and service technicians	50,900	462	39,100	12,976	76.8	25.5
Automotive body and related repairers	36,000	1,202	(B)	(B)	(X)	(X)
Automotive glass installers and repairers	33,300	4,512	(B)	(B)	(X)	(X)
Automotive service technicians and mechanics	34,600	745	26,700	5,488	77.2	15.9
Bus and truck mechanics and diesel engine specialists	40,300	403	(B)	(B)	(X)	(X)
Heavy vehicle and mobile equipment service technicians and mechanics	44,100	1,587	(B)	(B)	(X)	(X)
Small engine mechanics	31,500	1,759	(B)	(B)	(X)	(X)
Miscellaneous vehicle and mobile equipment mechanics, installers, and repairers	25,300	714	(B)	(B)	(X)	(X)
Control and valve installers and repairers	44,000	3,701	(B)	(B)	(X)	(X)
Heating, air conditioning, and refrigeration mechanics and installers	39,800	1,319	(B)	(B)	(X)	(X)
Home appliance repairers	35,600	1,160	(B)	(B)	(X)	(X)
Industrial and refractory machinery mechanics	45,600	299	38,500	4,099	84.3	9.0
Maintenance and repair workers, general	40,400	299	32,600	3,000	80.7	7.5
Maintenance workers, machinery	42,700	3,152	(B)	(B)	(X)	(X)
Millwrights	50,600	564	(B)	(B)	(X)	(X)
Electrical power-line installers and repairers	56,100	1,939	(B)	(B)	(X)	(X)
Telecommunications line installers and repairers	46,600	2,324	46,400	8,712	99.5	19.3
Precision instrument and equipment repairers	46,200	3,149	(B)	(B)	(X)	(X)
Coin, vending, and amusement machine servicers and repairers	31,300	1,642	(B)	(B)	(X)	(X)
Locksmiths and safe repairers	37,100	4,843	(B)	(B)	(X)	(X)
Riggers	43,700	4,481	(B)	(B)	(X)	(X)
Helpers—installation, maintenance, and repair workers	22,500	1,995	(B)	(B)	(X)	(X)
Other installation, maintenance, and repair workers	36,000	1,324	35,500	6,384	98.6	18.1
Production Occupations						
First-line supervisors/managers of production and operating workers	50,200	334	35,700	431	71.2	1.0
Electrical, electronics, and electromechanical assemblers	30,700	939	24,100	893	78.5	3.8
Engine and other machine assemblers	36,600	4,144	(B)	(B)	(X)	(X)
Structural metal fabricators and fitters	39,000	3,053	(B)	(B)	(X)	(X)
Miscellaneous assemblers and fabricators	30,800	156	24,600	595	80.0	2.0
Bakers	26,400	821	20,600	1,054	78.0	4.7
Butchers and other meat, poultry, and fish processing workers	26,700	1,112	20,400	520	76.3	3.7
Food batchmakers	29,400	1,879	22,300	1,925	75.8	8.1
Computer control programmers and operators	40,100	1,661	(B)	(B)	(X)	(X)
Extruding and drawing machine setters, operators, and tenders, metal and plastic	33,800	3,458	(B)	(B)	(X)	(X)

See footnotes at end of table.

Table A-2.
Median Earnings in the Past 12 Months of Workers by Sex and Women's Earnings as a Percentage of Men's Earnings by Detailed Occupation for the United States: 2007—Con.

(In 2007 inflation-adjusted dollars. For information on confidentiality protection, sampling error, nonsampling error, and definitions, see www.census.gov/acs/www/)

Occupation	Median earnings (dollars)				Women's earnings as a percentage of men's earnings[1]	
	Men		Women			
	Estimate	Margin of error[2] (±)	Estimate	Margin of error[2] (±)	Estimate	Margin of error[2] (±)
Production Occupations—Con.						
Forging machine setters, operators, and tenders, metal and plastic	36,500	1,989	(B)	(B)	(X)	(X)
Rolling machine setters, operators, and tenders, metal and plastic	35,700	1,477	(B)	(B)	(X)	(X)
Cutting, punching, and press machine setters, operators, and tenders, metal and plastic	30,700	926	24,500	1,798	79.7	6.3
Grinding, lapping, polishing, and buffing machine tool setters, operators, and tenders, metal and plastic	30,800	1,612	(B)	(B)	(X)	(X)
Lathe and turning machine tool setters, operators, and tenders, metal and plastic	34,500	4,877	(B)	(B)	(X)	(X)
Machinists	41,000	229	28,700	2,069	70.0	5.1
Metal furnace and kiln operators and tenders	40,100	2,244	(B)	(B)	(X)	(X)
Molders and molding machine setters, operators, and tenders, metal and plastic	35,500	1,566	25,200	3,318	70.8	9.8
Tool and die makers	50,600	413	(B)	(B)	(X)	(X)
Welding, soldering, and brazing workers	35,200	480	25,400	403	72.2	1.5
Plating and coating machine setters, operators, and tenders, metal and plastic	28,900	3,308	(B)	(B)	(X)	(X)
Tool grinders, filers, and sharpeners	37,600	3,826	(B)	(B)	(X)	(X)
Metalworkers and plastic workers, all other	33,500	1,036	24,600	628	73.4	2.9
Bookbinders and bindery workers	33,400	2,191	25,600	1,619	76.4	7.0
Job printers	32,800	4,516	26,200	1,291	79.8	11.7
Prepress technicians and workers	40,300	3,162	27,700	3,570	68.8	10.4
Printing machine operators	37,000	1,622	24,600	1,451	66.5	4.9
Laundry and dry-cleaning workers	22,400	1,349	17,500	1,179	77.8	7.0
Pressers, textile, garment, and related materials	20,900	1,813	16,700	729	80.1	7.8
Sewing machine operators	20,600	1,061	18,600	1,158	90.0	7.3
Shoe and leather workers and repairers	27,300	3,405	(B)	(B)	(X)	(X)
Tailors, dressmakers, and sewers	29,400	3,974	22,500	1,364	76.5	11.3
Upholsterers	27,100	2,152	(B)	(B)	(X)	(X)
Textile, apparel, and furnishings workers, all other	28,700	3,816	(B)	(B)	(X)	(X)
Cabinetmakers and bench carpenters	30,600	674	(B)	(B)	(X)	(X)
Furniture finishers	30,400	3,540	(B)	(B)	(X)	(X)
Sawing machine setters, operators, and tenders, wood	25,200	1,181	(B)	(B)	(X)	(X)
Woodworking machine setters, operators, and tenders, except sawing	28,300	3,532	(B)	(B)	(X)	(X)
Woodworkers, all other	28,800	2,949	(B)	(B)	(X)	(X)
Power plant operators, distributors, and dispatchers	71,600	1,209	(B)	(B)	(X)	(X)
Stationary engineers and boiler operators	50,800	640	(B)	(B)	(X)	(X)
Water and liquid waste treatment plant and system operators	40,600	683	(B)	(B)	(X)	(X)
Miscellaneous plant and system operators	56,600	4,532	(B)	(B)	(X)	(X)
Chemical processing machine setters, operators, and tenders	51,100	1,189	(B)	(B)	(X)	(X)
Crushing, grinding, polishing, mixing, and blending workers	34,200	1,716	25,700	6,365	75.0	19.0
Cutting workers	28,700	1,798	21,500	1,357	75.0	6.7
Extruding, forming, pressing, and compacting machine setters, operators, and tenders	32,800	1,500	(B)	(B)	(X)	(X)
Furnace, kiln, oven, drier, and kettle operators and tenders	40,900	6,134	(B)	(B)	(X)	(X)

See footnotes at end of table.

Table A-2.
Median Earnings in the Past 12 Months of Workers by Sex and Women's Earnings as a Percentage of Men's Earnings by Detailed Occupation for the United States: 2007—Con.

(In 2007 inflation-adjusted dollars. For information on confidentiality protection, sampling error, nonsampling error, and definitions, see www.census.gov/acs/www/)

| Occupation | Median earnings (dollars) | | | | Women's earnings as a percentage of men's earnings[1] | |
| | Men | | Women | | | |
	Estimate	Margin of error[2] (±)	Estimate	Margin of error[2] (±)	Estimate	Margin of error[2] (±)
Production Occupations—Con.						
Inspectors, testers, sorters, samplers, and weighers	41,100	326	28,200	791	68.7	2.0
Jewelers and precious stone and metal workers	32,300	2,160	25,300	4,167	78.3	13.9
Medical, dental, and ophthalmic laboratory technicians	38,100	3,255	30,100	1,726	79.0	8.1
Packaging and filling machine operators and tenders	26,400	1,691	20,500	398	77.9	5.2
Painting workers	32,100	1,355	22,400	1,219	69.8	4.8
Photographic process workers and processing machine operators	29,500	5,606	20,400	604	69.1	13.3
Molders, shapers, and casters, except metal and plastic	30,500	1,199	(B)	(B)	(X)	(X)
Paper goods machine setters, operators, and tenders	41,100	3,163	22,400	2,249	54.4	6.9
Tire builders	41,100	12,635	(B)	(B)	(X)	(X)
Helpers—production workers	25,100	1,425	(B)	(B)	(X)	(X)
Production workers, all other	32,900	521	25,300	163	77.0	1.3
Transportation and Material Moving Occupations						
Supervisors, transportation and material moving workers	46,900	2,532	35,600	957	76.0	4.6
Aircraft pilots and flight engineers	87,100	6,763	(B)	(B)	(X)	(X)
Air traffic controllers and airfield operations specialists	77,000	11,030	(B)	(B)	(X)	(X)
Bus drivers	34,800	977	25,400	387	73.0	2.3
Driver/sales workers and truck drivers	38,900	313	28,200	2,032	72.5	5.3
Taxi drivers and chauffeurs	26,400	918	21,500	1,716	81.7	7.1
Motor vehicle operators, all other	23,300	3,348	(B)	(B)	(X)	(X)
Locomotive engineers and operators	66,700	1,364	(B)	(B)	(X)	(X)
Railroad brake, signal, and switch operators	48,700	6,962	(B)	(B)	(X)	(X)
Railroad conductors and yardmasters	60,600	2,648	(B)	(B)	(X)	(X)
Sailors and marine oilers	35,200	1,546	(B)	(B)	(X)	(X)
Ship and boat captains and operators	51,000	5,116	(B)	(B)	(X)	(X)
Parking lot attendants	22,200	3,473	(B)	(B)	(X)	(X)
Service station attendants	21,100	1,130	17,900	1,479	84.7	8.4
Transportation inspectors	55,100	2,645	(B)	(B)	(X)	(X)
Other transportation workers	35,000	4,034	(B)	(B)	(X)	(X)
Crane and tower operators	50,600	823	(B)	(B)	(X)	(X)
Dredge, excavating, and loading machine operators	38,000	2,569	(B)	(B)	(X)	(X)
Industrial truck and tractor operators	29,400	714	28,100	1,594	95.8	5.9
Cleaners of vehicles and equipment	22,300	1,166	20,300	637	90.9	5.5
Laborers and freight, stock, and material movers, hand ...	28,400	308	23,300	489	82.0	1.9
Machine feeders and offbearers	28,700	3,130	20,500	2,393	71.3	11.4
Packers and packagers, hand	23,300	1,380	20,200	202	86.7	5.2
Pumping station operators	46,100	2,938	(B)	(B)	(X)	(X)
Refuse and recyclable material collectors	29,300	2,706	(B)	(B)	(X)	(X)
Material moving workers, all other	35,400	2,449	(B)	(B)	(X)	(X)

(B) Less than 100 sample cases. Base figure too small to meet statistical standards for reliability of a derived figure.
(X) Not applicable.

[1] Ratios calculated from unrounded data.
[2] Data are based on a sample and are subject to sampling variability. A margin of error is a measure of an estimate's variability. The larger the margin of error in relation to the size of the estimate, the less reliable the estimate. When added to and subtracted from the estimate, the margin of error forms the 90-percent confidence interval.

Source: U.S. Census Bureau, 2007 American Community Survey.

Figure B-1.
Percentage of People in Poverty in the Past 12 Months With Margins of Error by State: 2007

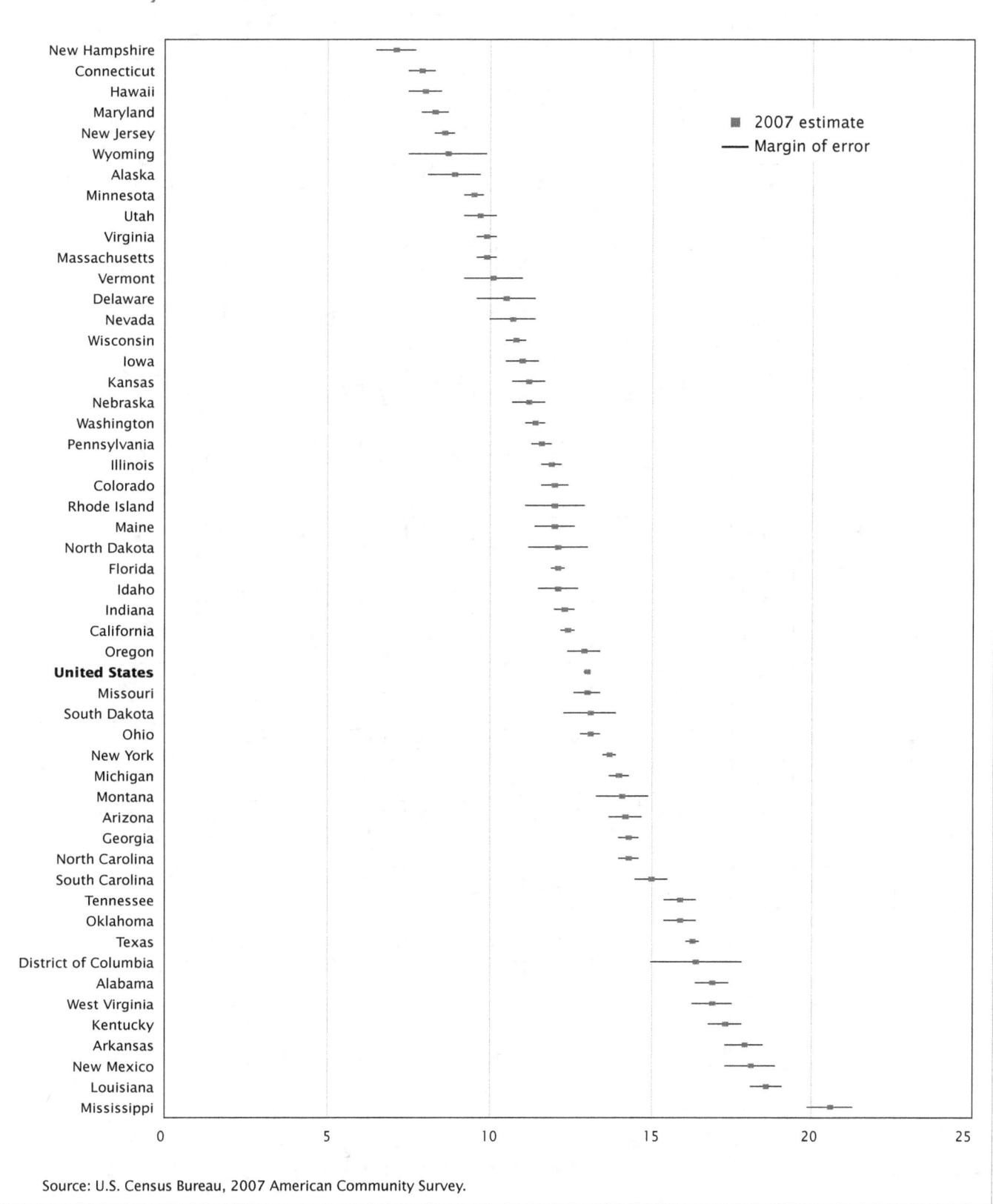

Source: U.S. Census Bureau, 2007 American Community Survey.

Percentage of People Below Poverty Level in the Past 12 Months by Metropolitan or Micropolitan Statistical Area Status and State: 2007

(For information on confidentiality protection, sampling error, nonsampling error, and definitions, see www.census.gov/acs/www/)

Area	Total		In metropolitan or micropolitan statistical area												Not in metropolitan or micropolitan statistical area	
			In metropolitan statistical area						In micropolitan statistical area							
			Total		In principal city		Not in principal city		Total		In principal city		Not in principal city			
	Percentage[1]	Margin of error[2] (±)	Percentage[1]	Margin of error[2] (±)	Percentage[1]	Margin of error[2] (±)	Percentage[1]	Margin of error[2] (±)	Percentage[1]	Margin of error[2] (±)	Percentage[1]	Margin of error[2] (±)	Percentage[1]	Margin of error[2] (±)	Percentage[1]	Margin of error[2] (±)
United States	12.7	0.1	12.4	0.1	17.2	0.1	9.4	0.1	15.4	0.2	20.1	0.3	13.1	0.2	16.6	0.2
Alabama	16.3	0.5	16.0	0.6	19.8	1.0	13.7	0.7	17.9	1.1	21.8	2.1	16.2	1.3	21.3	1.6
Alaska	7.2	0.9	7.4	1.0	7.2	1.2	7.9	1.7	(B)	(B)	(B)	(B)	(B)	(B)	14.5	1.3
Arizona	13.7	0.5	13.6	0.5	15.5	0.7	11.2	0.7	17.7	2.3	18.3	4.5	17.3	2.4	26.8	2.4
Arkansas	17.3	0.7	16.5	0.8	19.0	1.5	14.3	0.9	20.0	1.3	24.0	2.4	17.9	1.6	20.0	1.4
California	12.4	0.2	12.4	0.2	13.9	0.3	10.9	0.3	14.9	1.5	18.0	2.9	13.8	1.8	12.9	1.7
Colorado	11.8	0.4	11.8	0.5	16.6	0.8	8.1	0.6	12.4	1.9	17.9	4.0	9.9	2.3	13.8	1.4
Connecticut	7.9	0.4	8.1	0.4	13.8	1.0	5.6	0.4	6.1	0.9	(B)	(B)	4.4	0.9	(X)	(X)
Delaware	10.5	0.9	10.8	1.0	23.6	4.2	8.6	1.0	9.2	1.4	(B)	(B)	9.0	1.4	(X)	(X)
District of Columbia	16.4	1.4	16.4	1.4	16.4	1.4	(X)	(X)	(X)	(X)	(X)	(X)	(X)	(X)	(X)	(X)
Florida	12.0	0.2	11.9	0.2	15.1	0.5	10.7	0.2	14.9	1.3	12.7	2.6	15.3	1.5	17.7	1.9
Georgia	13.8	0.4	13.1	0.4	21.8	1.0	10.8	0.4	19.9	1.2	27.6	2.5	16.3	1.4	19.2	1.4
Hawaii	8.0	0.5	7.6	0.7	8.6	1.1	7.0	0.9	8.8	1.1	10.8	2.7	8.2	1.3	(B)	(B)
Idaho	11.9	0.7	11.1	0.8	12.0	1.1	10.3	1.2	14.4	1.6	18.2	2.5	12.3	1.8	13.7	1.9
Illinois	11.9	0.3	11.7	0.3	17.7	0.5	7.8	0.3	14.5	0.7	20.6	1.5	11.1	0.9	12.7	0.9
Indiana	12.4	0.3	12.3	0.4	18.0	0.7	8.6	0.4	12.5	0.8	17.2	1.6	10.0	0.8	11.9	1.4
Iowa	11.5	0.5	11.1	0.6	15.9	1.0	5.6	0.6	12.7	1.2	15.9	1.9	9.0	1.3	9.8	0.8
Kansas	11.4	0.5	10.3	0.6	14.3	0.9	6.5	0.7	14.5	1.1	16.6	1.6	11.6	1.4	10.1	0.9
Kentucky	15.5	0.6	14.0	0.6	17.1	1.0	11.9	0.7	20.3	1.5	23.0	2.3	19.3	1.9	23.0	1.3
Louisiana	18.2	0.5	16.8	0.5	20.7	1.2	14.1	0.7	23.8	1.3	30.5	2.8	21.0	1.4	24.1	2.0
Maine	10.8	0.8	10.5	0.9	14.8	2.0	9.1	1.0	12.1	1.9	(B)	(B)	8.2	1.5	15.1	1.1
Maryland	8.2	0.4	8.2	0.4	16.0	1.0	6.4	0.4	8.1	1.6	(B)	(B)	6.9	1.7	12.7	2.5
Massachusetts	10.0	0.3	10.0	0.3	17.2	0.8	7.5	0.3	(X)	(X)	(X)	(X)	(X)	(X)	(B)	(B)
Michigan	13.9	0.3	13.9	0.3	23.4	0.6	9.4	0.3	13.9	0.7	21.5	1.8	11.9	0.7	15.3	0.7
Minnesota	9.3	0.3	9.1	0.3	14.7	0.7	6.6	0.4	10.3	0.7	13.8	1.3	7.8	0.7	10.9	0.7
Mississippi	19.4	0.7	15.5	1.0	23.3	2.1	12.7	1.0	24.5	1.2	30.7	2.3	20.9	1.6	24.8	1.6
Missouri	12.3	0.4	11.8	0.4	18.7	1.0	8.9	0.4	15.1	1.1	19.8	2.0	12.4	1.1	17.7	1.1
Montana	13.1	1.0	12.6	1.3	14.1	1.8	9.8	2.0	13.6	1.7	19.0	3.1	10.2	2.2	16.2	1.4
Nebraska	11.0	0.5	10.6	0.7	13.6	1.1	6.0	0.8	11.9	1.1	14.0	1.6	9.2	1.3	12.2	0.9
Nevada	10.6	0.7	10.5	0.7	12.0	1.0	9.1	0.8	11.7	2.4	12.4	3.7	11.3	2.8	(B)	(B)
New Hampshire	6.9	0.6	6.4	0.7	10.6	2.2	5.1	0.7	7.9	0.9	9.1	2.0	7.5	0.9	(B)	(B)

See footnotes at end of table.

Table B-1.
Percentage of People Below Poverty Level in the Past 12 Months by Metropolitan or Micropolitan Statistical Area Status and State: 2007—Con.

(For information on confidentiality protection, sampling error, nonsampling error, and definitions, see www.census.gov/acs/www/)

Area	Total		In metropolitan or micropolitan statistical area												Not in metropolitan or micropolitan statistical area	
			In metropolitan statistical area						In micropolitan statistical area							
			Total		In principal city		Not in principal city		Total		In principal city		Not in principal city			
	Percentage[1]	Margin of error[2] (±)	Percentage[1]	Margin of error[2] (±)	Percentage[1]	Margin of error[2] (±)	Percentage[1]	Margin of error[2] (±)	Percentage[1]	Margin of error[2] (±)	Percentage[1]	Margin of error[2] (±)	Percentage[1]	Margin of error[2] (±)	Percentage[1]	Margin of error[2] (±)
New Jersey	8.6	0.3	8.6	0.3	19.0	1.4	7.5	0.3	(X)	(X)	(X)	(X)	(X)	(X)	(X)	(X)
New Mexico	17.9	0.9	16.8	1.0	16.5	1.3	17.1	1.5	20.2	1.6	20.4	2.0	20.1	2.3	24.3	3.7
New York	13.7	0.2	13.7	0.2	19.3	0.4	6.9	0.2	14.2	0.8	21.1	2.3	11.9	0.7	12.8	1.0
North Carolina	13.9	0.3	13.2	0.4	15.9	0.7	11.2	0.4	16.2	0.7	21.8	1.7	14.4	0.8	18.6	1.3
North Dakota	11.6	1.1	12.3	1.3	15.5	1.8	6.3	1.7	10.2	1.6	11.0	2.3	(B)	(B)	13.2	1.2
Ohio	13.1	0.3	13.0	0.3	23.4	0.8	8.9	0.3	13.4	0.6	20.0	1.6	10.8	0.5	14.2	1.3
Oklahoma	15.3	0.5	14.3	0.6	17.6	1.0	11.7	0.8	18.2	1.1	22.2	1.9	13.5	1.2	19.6	1.2
Oregon	12.8	0.5	12.4	0.6	14.7	0.8	10.6	0.7	14.3	1.1	17.7	2.1	12.4	1.2	17.0	2.6
Pennsylvania	11.6	0.3	11.5	0.3	23.7	0.9	7.6	0.2	12.1	0.6	22.2	2.3	10.4	0.6	13.3	1.1
Rhode Island	12.0	0.9	12.0	0.9	18.2	2.3	9.2	0.9	(X)	(X)	(X)	(X)	(X)	(X)	(X)	(X)
South Carolina	14.4	0.5	13.7	0.5	18.5	1.3	12.6	0.5	17.3	1.3	18.3	2.7	17.1	1.4	25.1	2.7
South Dakota	10.8	0.9	9.1	1.1	11.4	1.7	5.8	1.4	13.7	1.5	16.9	1.8	8.9	2.3	19.2	1.8
Tennessee	15.5	0.5	15.0	0.5	19.6	0.9	11.0	0.5	17.6	1.0	25.0	2.2	15.0	1.1	19.8	1.5
Texas	16.2	0.2	16.0	0.2	19.5	0.3	12.0	0.4	19.4	1.1	23.0	1.6	16.0	1.3	17.5	1.0
Utah	9.4	0.5	9.1	0.5	17.3	1.4	6.2	0.6	13.8	2.0	16.6	3.7	11.5	2.5	14.6	2.1
Vermont	9.2	1.0	7.9	1.4	(B)	(B)	6.0	1.3	10.2	1.3	(B)	(B)	9.1	1.3	12.6	1.5
Virginia	9.3	0.3	9.1	0.3	14.0	0.6	6.9	0.3	13.8	1.7	18.9	4.1	11.8	2.0	15.2	1.1
Washington	11.2	0.3	10.9	0.3	14.5	0.7	8.9	0.4	14.9	1.1	21.8	2.4	11.8	1.3	16.9	1.8
West Virginia	16.0	0.8	14.9	1.1	20.4	2.4	13.4	1.1	19.0	1.6	26.8	4.1	16.8	1.8	19.6	1.5
Wisconsin	10.7	0.4	10.9	0.4	18.0	0.8	6.5	0.4	9.8	0.8	16.1	1.8	7.3	0.7	11.4	0.7
Wyoming	8.2	1.3	6.8	1.6	6.5	1.9	(B)	(B)	9.1	1.9	8.6	1.7	9.8	3.4	9.9	2.4
Puerto Rico	45.4	0.7	45.0	0.7	41.7	1.3	46.1	0.8	55.8	3.7	(B)	(B)	53.1	4.6	(B)	(B)

(B) Data for territories below the population of 65,000 are not published as single-year estimates by the American Community Survey.
(X) Not applicable. Indicates states that do not contain any territory in micropolitan statistical areas and/or do not contain any territory outside of metropolitan or micropolitan statistical areas.
[1] Poverty status is determined for individuals in housing units and noninstitutional group quarters except people living in college dormitories or military barracks. Unrelated individuals under 15 years old are also excluded from the poverty universe.
[2] Data are based on a sample and are subject to sampling variability. A margin of error is a measure of an estimate's variability. The larger the margin of error in relation to the size of the estimate, the less reliable the estimate. When added to and subtracted from the estimate, the margin of error forms the 90-percent confidence interval.

Source: U.S. Census Bureau, 2007 American Community Survey and 2007 Puerto Rico Community Survey.

Table B-2.
Number and Percentage of People by Income-to-Poverty Ratio in the Past 12 Months by State: 2007

(For information on confidentiality protection, sampling error, nonsampling error, and definitions, see *www.census.gov/acs/www/*)

Area	All people for whom poverty status is determined[1] (thousands)	Percentage of people with income-to-poverty ratio less than—					
		50 percent		100 percent		125 percent	
		Estimate	Margin of error[2] (±)	Estimate	Margin of error[2] (±)	Estimate	Margin of error[2] (±)
United States	293,744	5.6	0.1	13.0	0.1	17.3	0.1
Alabama	4,507	6.9	0.3	16.9	0.5	22.0	0.5
Alaska	667	3.7	0.5	8.9	0.8	13.3	1.0
Arizona	6,225	6.6	0.3	14.2	0.5	18.9	0.5
Arkansas	2,754	6.5	0.4	17.9	0.6	23.5	0.7
California	35,768	5.1	0.1	12.4	0.2	17.3	0.2
Colorado	4,756	5.5	0.3	12.0	0.4	15.7	0.5
Connecticut	3,388	3.6	0.3	7.9	0.4	10.7	0.4
Delaware	838	5.2	0.6	10.5	0.9	14.3	1.0
District of Columbia	560	8.5	1.1	16.4	1.4	20.6	1.4
Florida	17,847	5.0	0.1	12.1	0.2	16.7	0.3
Georgia	9,286	6.4	0.3	14.3	0.3	18.8	0.4
Hawaii	1,255	3.8	0.4	8.0	0.5	10.5	0.6
Idaho	1,464	4.7	0.5	12.1	0.6	17.1	0.7
Illinois	12,541	5.3	0.2	11.9	0.3	15.8	0.3
Indiana	6,145	5.8	0.3	12.3	0.3	16.4	0.4
Iowa	2,882	4.7	0.3	11.0	0.5	14.7	0.5
Kansas	2,689	4.8	0.3	11.2	0.5	15.2	0.5
Kentucky	4,121	7.1	0.3	17.3	0.5	22.0	0.5
Louisiana	4,167	7.8	0.4	18.6	0.5	24.1	0.6
Maine	1,281	4.6	0.4	12.0	0.6	16.4	0.7
Maryland	5,478	3.8	0.2	8.3	0.4	11.0	0.4
Massachusetts	6,245	4.4	0.2	9.9	0.3	12.7	0.3
Michigan	9,833	6.5	0.2	14.0	0.3	18.2	0.3
Minnesota	5,067	3.9	0.2	9.5	0.3	12.7	0.3
Mississippi	2,822	8.7	0.5	20.6	0.7	27.1	0.8
Missouri	5,709	5.7	0.3	13.0	0.4	17.6	0.4
Montana	933	5.8	0.6	14.1	0.8	19.1	1.0
Nebraska	1,719	4.8	0.4	11.2	0.5	15.7	0.6
Nevada	2,529	4.6	0.3	10.7	0.7	14.1	0.8
New Hampshire	1,275	3.4	0.4	7.1	0.6	9.8	0.7
New Jersey	8,506	3.9	0.2	8.6	0.3	11.4	0.3
New Mexico	1,926	7.6	0.5	18.1	0.8	23.5	0.9
New York	18,775	6.1	0.2	13.7	0.2	17.7	0.2
North Carolina	8,793	6.0	0.2	14.3	0.3	19.4	0.3
North Dakota	613	5.3	0.6	12.1	0.9	15.7	0.9
Ohio	11,151	6.0	0.2	13.1	0.3	17.3	0.3
Oklahoma	3,498	6.7	0.3	15.9	0.5	21.4	0.6
Oregon	3,670	5.7	0.4	12.9	0.5	17.6	0.6
Pennsylvania	11,999	5.1	0.2	11.6	0.3	15.6	0.3
Rhode Island	1,019	5.2	0.7	12.0	0.9	15.5	1.0
South Carolina	4,270	6.7	0.3	15.0	0.5	20.2	0.5
South Dakota	768	5.6	0.6	13.1	0.8	17.8	0.8
Tennessee	5,997	6.5	0.3	15.9	0.5	20.7	0.5
Texas	23,284	6.8	0.2	16.3	0.2	21.8	0.2
Utah	2,601	3.8	0.3	9.7	0.5	13.7	0.6
Vermont	600	3.9	0.4	10.1	0.9	14.2	0.9
Virginia	7,466	4.2	0.2	9.9	0.3	13.1	0.3
Washington	6,338	5.1	0.3	11.4	0.3	15.2	0.4
West Virginia	1,763	7.0	0.5	16.9	0.6	22.6	0.7
Wisconsin	5,447	4.5	0.2	10.8	0.3	14.6	0.4
Wyoming	509	3.6	0.8	8.7	1.2	11.8	1.2
Puerto Rico	3,878	26.0	0.6	45.5	0.7	54.1	0.7

[1] Poverty status is determined for individuals in housing units and noninstitutional group quarters except people living in college dormitories or military barracks. Unrelated individuals under 15 years old are also excluded from the poverty universe.
[2] Data are based on a sample and are subject to sampling variability. A margin of error is a measure of an estimate's variability. The larger the margin of error in relation to the size of the estimate, the less reliable the estimate. When added to and subtracted from the estimate, the margin of error forms the 90-percent confidence interval.

Source: U.S. Census Bureau, 2007 American Community Survey and 2007 Puerto Rico Community Survey.